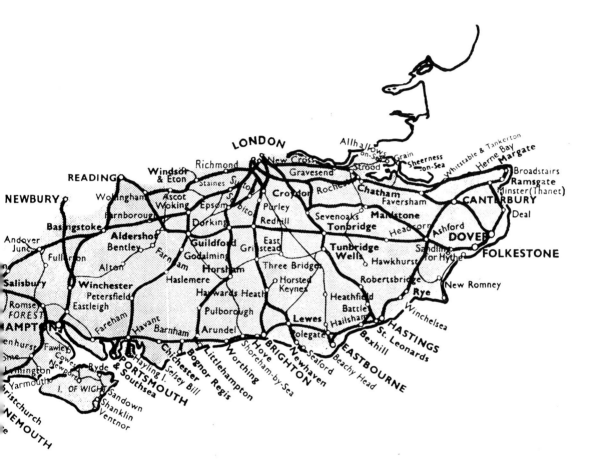

RAIL ROVER
FROM KENT TO CORNWALL

Earliest known portrait of the author in a railway environment: in the late-afternoon sunshine, during a family holiday in the West Country in August 1950, 'Small Prairie' 2–6-2T no. 5569 was discovered with the Launceston–Plymouth pick-up goods at Tavistock (South). All evidence of this former Great Western Railway station, with its Brunel-style overall roof, has now vanished along with the antiquated cattle vans and typical branch line steam locomotive, but when aged thirteen one never expected it all to disappear. (J. Barber Glenn.)

RAIL ROVER
FROM KENT TO CORNWALL

D. FEREDAY GLENN

SUTTON PUBLISHING

Alan Sutton Publishing Limited
an imprint of Sutton Publishing Limited
Phoenix Mill · Thrupp · Stroud · Gloucestershire

First Published 1988
Reprinted 1997
Copyright © D. Fereday Glenn 1988
Copyright © photographs D. Fereday Glenn 1988,
unless otherwise credited.

British Library Cataloguing in Publication Data

Fereday – Glenn, D. (David)
Rail Rover.
1. Great Britain. Rural regions. Rail
travel – Personal observations.
I. Title
385′.22′0924

ISBN 0-86299-530-2

Jacket illustrations: Front: Built by the LBSCR in 1880, Alx 'Terrier'
0-6-0T 32678 raises the echoes as it makes a noisy departure from
Langston with the branch train to Hayling Island. *Back:* Hampshire
three-car diesel-electric multiple unit 1103 is framed by trees as it heads
northwards from Fareham towards Funtley tunnel on the single line
through Knowle Halt to Botley and Eastleigh. (Photographs: D. Fereday
Glenn)

Typesetting and origination by
Alan Sutton Publishing Limited.
Printed in Great Britain by
Dotesios Printers Limited.

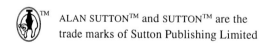

'One's whole life is devoted to re-creating the past
and making it live'

SIR MORTIMER WHEELER

CONTENTS

At 1.05 p.m. sharp Class S15 4–6–0 no. 30832 rolls its heavy freight for Templecombe out of Salisbury West Yard, watched by Courtney Haydon, on 4 October 1958. The locomotive depot (72B) is immediately behind the photographer.

ACKNOWLEDGEMENTS

It is only right that I should pay tribute to my old school friend, John Courtney Haydon, with whom I shared a number of holidays and rail journeys from the mid-1950s onwards and who has been a most generous godfather to my two sons. I should also like to thank British Railways for the use of publicity material; Margaret Lovell for her unfailing patience and interest when checking manuscripts; and my parents for their tolerance of a hobby that can manifest itself in any scale between 4mm and 12 inches to the foot! To them, and to all the un-named railwaymen whose kindness has contributed greatly to my appreciation of their work behind the scenes, a very sincere 'Thank You'. Finally, a thought for the late C. Hamilton Ellis, whose article in *Trains Illustrated* while I was at school inspired my enthusiasm to seek out the aged Beattie well-tanks in North Cornwall.

D. Fereday Glenn
Catisfield, England
January 1988

INTRODUCTION

———

When I first went to boarding school it was very much a case of 'Six days shalt thou labour'. Mondays to Saturdays, inclusive, were for lessons, organised games and homework – with occasional pauses for food – but on Sundays, apart from attendance at church and completion of the weekly letter home, life was pretty well what one made it. Looking out over the playing fields, right from my first day, could be seen the embankment that carried the railway line from Petersfield to Midhurst. It curved away into the distance, lost among the trees in Durford Wood, and when the little train appeared it seemed to scurry along that embankment with remarkable speed. As days passed into weeks, and weeks into months, I came to know more and more about the ways of that rural byway of the newly-formed British Railways: sometimes the carriages were red, at other times they were green, but always the engine was black. Every weekday a goods train ran once in each direction, and soon I learned the times of each service until it almost became an arithmetical table. Early and late, one could hear the train crossing Ramshill bridge from the comfort of a bed in the dormitory, while during the day it was sometimes possible to see it from the classroom window as it emerged from the trees and bustled along the tall embankment beyond Love Lane. But after lunch on Sundays, when pupils were required to go for walks until tea, I could escape through the gates out into the real world beyond – and find the train!

The main station building at Petersfield was, and happily still is, one of those distinctive structures designed for the opening of the Portsmouth Direct railway line in 1859. However, it took no more than a single visit to discover that the little Midhurst train (known to all as 'The Middy') seldom used it. Rather, it was tucked away with its own simple platform on the other side of the A272 road, to the north of the level crossing gates,

———

In the early years of British Railways, former LBSCR passenger tank engines could be found alternating with LSWR varieties on 'The Middy'. Built in the final decade of the Victorian Age Billinton Class D3 0–4–4T no. 32364 bustles along the single line with a Petersfield to Midhurst motor train not far from Elstead *c.* 1950. (D. Fereday Glenn collection, courtesy of E.C. Griffith.)

One of the very few souvenir pictures of the Petersfield to Midhurst line obtained by the author in his final year at Churcher's College. On a murky winter day, E5x 0–6–2T no. 32576 headed the return working of the goods to Midhurst and Pulborough in the loop platform at Petersfield station on Saturday, 22 January 1955, just a fortnight before total closure of the former LSWR branch. While most passenger services operated from their own bay platform opposite the signal box, on the north side of the A272 level crossing, the Midhurst branch freight buffered up to a Guildford-bound goods in the main station. The main line freight departed about 1.15 p.m., while the E5x had to wait until 1.35 p.m. to obtain a clear path.

opposite the signal box. Fleet of foot though I was, the train got there first: carriage doors stood open invitingly, but it was not possible to have a ride. Even if I had been able to save up enough pocket money to buy a return ticket, the service was sparse; had I boarded the 15.19 to any of the intermediate stations, there was no train back to Petersfield until 19.07, long after roll-call, tea and evensong. Perhaps because the timetable had not been compiled with pupils like me in mind, it was more than six years before I was able to experience a trip with 'The Middy' – and then it took place during the school holidays – being prompted by imminent closure of 'our' line by faceless officials somewhere in London, the Sunday service having been an earlier casualty. I did have one more ride over the

Anyone passing over the footbridge alongside the level crossing would have had this view of the Midhurst bay platform at Petersfield. With the crossing gates closed to road traffic and the branch train anxious to leave, only a connecting service from Portsmouth is awaited. The milk churns on the platform provide the finishing touch to this delightful study of a morning train c. 1950. The train itself is an all-LSWR outfit consisting of a Drummond M7 0–4–4T and two-coach corridor push-pull set no. 737. (D. Fereday Glenn collection, courtesy of E.C. Griffith.)

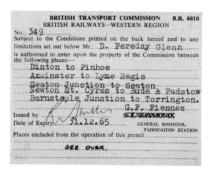

Evidence of the transfer of responsibility for lines west of Salisbury to the Western Region is provided by this photographic permit for 1965. All the routes for which facilities had been granted were former Southern lines, and only 'Dinton to Pinhoe' remains open to all traffic.

INTRODUCTION

branch before it closed: in my capacity as Chairman of the College Railway Club, overtures to the headmaster for an outing to Midhurst on the last day were favourably received. It was a strangely sad occasion that Saturday afternoon of 5 February 1955. Though the sun came out while we stood about in little groups on the platform, waiting for the engine to run round its train (specially lengthened to three coaches for the unaccustomed patronage), the solemnity and finality touched us all. Until then, it had not seemed possible to imagine life without 'The Middy', so much a part of the curriculum had it become, but then the realisation dawned that next Monday none of us would be roused from our slumbers just before the rising bell by the shrill whistle of a 50-year-old Drummond M7.

The last day. Members of the College Railway Club pose for the Chairman's camera at Midhurst shortly after arrival of the 14.50 train from Petersfield on Saturday, 5 February 1955. M7 0–4–4T no. 30028 stands at the buffer stops of the bay platform, attached to push-pull set 653, while an additional ex-LBSCR carriage (out of the picture) was added to strengthen the train for this occasion.

A complete Edwardian train, still running in the 1950s! Built in 1903, M7 0–4–4T no. 30375 slakes its thirst at Fareham before continuing to Andover Junction (via Southampton) with the 11.19 stopping train from Portsmouth & Southsea on 12 April 1955. The three-coach train is a contemporary set of panelled non-corridor LSWR stock, with sliding doors to accommodate luggage in the commodious guard's compartment.

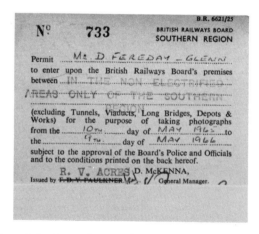

Last in a long line of Southern photographic permits; the expired permit had to be surrendered before a new one was issued by Waterloo.

One of the through services to be unaffected by modernisation in 1957 was the Brighton to Cardiff operation, seen leaving Fareham in fine style with three-cylinder Class U1 2–6–0 no. 31898 in charge on 2 March 1957. BR Standard Mk.I carriages were provided, painted in the attractive livery of Carmine and Cream ('Blood and Custard').

So ill-prepared was I for the end of that little railway that I didn't even get a new film for my camera to record it properly. But the lesson was learned for the future: in the course of the next twelve years I set out to chronicle as much of the passing railway scene as was practicable, given the limitations of my budget as a student and the means to travel long journeys to find quaint survivors of a bygone age. It became clear with the passage of time that officialdom's obsession with closure and the wholesale scrapping of steam locomotives was not just a bad dream that would cease if one woke up, or if there was a change of government. The great railway revolution that had overtaken the network of canals and coastal shipping throughout Britain in the nineteenth century was itself under seige from newer forms of technology – the bus, the lorry and, above all, the private car.

On leaving school I was articled to a solicitor in Portsmouth. This change in my circumstances meant daily commuting from the family home near Fareham, a journey that could be accomplished either by bus

Two-coach diesel-electric multiple unit no. 1113 approaches Fareham from the Netley line while working a semi-fast Salisbury–Portsmouth service on 15 March 1958. Early examples of these sets featured large route-indicator numerals at first, while most had an intermediate carriage added during 1959 to reduce overcrowding.

or by train. Though the former was easier in theory, in practice over-crowding by schoolchildren encouraged use of the latter. Not that I needed much arm-twisting with a weekly Runabout ticket costing only 15s. 0d. (75p), third class, and even a choice of area in which to travel! This freedom was, however, short-lived: after 31 October each year facilities appropriate to the holiday season were withdrawn, but it was marvellous while it lasted. Area No.8 offered tempting trips to places as far afield as Amberley or Littlehampton in the east to Winchester (City or Chesil) in the west, while Area No.16 operated between Portsmouth Harbour, Southampton (Terminus or Central), Romsey and either Andover Junction or Salisbury. While I was only able to utilize the Runabout ticket as a kind of cheap season from Monday to Friday, on Saturday and Sunday one was free to go to any of the other destinations as a bonus – and, incredibly, all trains from Fareham were steam-hauled!

Of course, modernisation was on the way in the shape of Eastleigh-built diesel-electric multiple units, which made their debut in traffic during the

INTRODUCTION

summer of 1957. Full implementation with regular interval operation began with the winter timetable, except for the Andover and Mid-Hants routes; they fell into line in November 1957. But not everything changed: the through trains between Brighton and Bournemouth, Cardiff or Plymouth continued with steam haulage, as did services between Portsmouth and Bristol or Cardiff. Freight trains still rumbled through or shunted in the yard as before, while additional van trains (for parcels and mail) had to be provided to shift the loads formerly moved by passenger services: the new diesels had too little space for such traffic and, with only two-car formations available initially, were soon overloaded in any case.

Where better to commence a railway journey than at a great London terminus? This 1957 scene at Charing Cross shows the 11.48 for Ashford (Kent) with Maunsell 'Schools' 4–4–0 no. 30929 *Malvern* waiting impatiently for the guard's flag, while alongside a train of several 2-HAL electric units is bound for Gillingham via Greenwich. The handsome 'V' Class locomotive has built up a good head of steam for the 56-mile journey via Tonbridge, and is shown freshly outshopped in 'top link' Brunswick Green livery.

INTRODUCTION

As a result, few of the older steam engines had to be withdrawn immediately.

The advent of the diesels served only to intensify the wish to travel more widely than a mere bicycle would allow. In 1958 with the help of a small legacy I was able to purchase a second-hand Lambretta 150cc scooter, which enlarged my horizons considerably. From that time on, visits to the more remote areas or to freight-only routes became possible at very modest cost – consumption of 2-stroke fuel was about 100m.p.g – without impairing the pleasure of rail travel wherever it remained feasible. Then, in 1959, availability of the Rail Rover ticket brought the entire Southern Region within scope for less than £1 per day. As the brochure said: 'If you enjoy a touring holiday this is the very ticket for you. Travel in comfort by train without the strain of keeping one eye on the road . . . You can go at any time except by Continental Boat Trains or Ocean Liner Expresses between London and Southampton.'

Just imagine – a train waiting at the platform, its doors swung open invitingly; step inside and take a seat. Whether diesel or electric multiple units, local services stopping at all stations or overnight journeys on the mail and newspaper trains to the far west, hauled by steam, the Rail Rover ticket opened up new vistas anywhere on the Southern Region between Kent and Cornwall. I was lucky enough to avail myself of this bargain-to-beat-all-bargains in 1959, 1960 and 1961, which I have sought in this volume to condense into a single week's travel. Will you come along too?

SOUTHERN RAILWAY
Issued subject to the Bye-laws, Regulations &
Conditions in the Company's Bills and Notices.

MONDAY

NOT TRANSFERABLE

TO ROYAL TUNBRIDGE WELLS
AND THE HOP-PICKERS' LINE

The brochure stated unequivocally: 'With a Rail Rover Ticket you can travel anywhere you like for seven whole days within this area . . . for only £6.' For an impecunious law student caught between courting and the Courts, such a prospect provided respite from both, and where better to 'start the week' than Fareham Railway Station on Monday, 10 August 1959? Having made a provisional itinerary for the day, I joined the morning commuters on Platform 2 to await an eastbound train. Essential equipment consisted of a holdall containing spare film, filters, etc., showerproof coat, basic rations and the current timetable; the camera was slung over the shoulder for instant use. Perhaps a word about the Southern Region timetable might not come amiss here, for it was more bulky than the current edition of the entire residue of British Rail. With appropriate green cover and including a useful map of the Region, with connecting lines, it cost a mere 1s. 0d. (5p). There were two issues each year, but the summer edition was always of greater interest since it featured additional seasonal trains that operated for limited periods only.

In 1959 I had just one camera, a Zeiss Ikon Nettar with 2¼ in. square format, purchased new in December 1956; it cost less than £12 including case. Being comparatively simple, it offered only three shutter speeds with a maximum of 1/200 second, coupled to a very modest lens aperture of f6.3, and was thus somewhat limited in its range. As you might expect from such specifications, it was not capable of 'stopping' an express

11

travelling at any real velocity close-to. This influenced my choice of subject matter and location, consciously or unconsciously, in favour of secondary or branch lines rather than well-known 'race-track' sections. Despite its limitations, the camera has been completely reliable and is still in use today for monochrome pictures – touch wood, it has never ceased to function and must have about 10,000 negatives to its credit by now. People sometimes laugh when they see its antique 'bellows' and manual shutter-cock mechanism, but the results speak for themselves. The chance to branch out into colour photography did not occur until later, for although my father purchased a neat little Kodak Retinette 1A 35mm camera to take transparencies in 1959, with very rare exceptions (such as finishing off a film) he would not permit me to get my hands on it.

Fondly remembered from the last day of the 'Middy', M7 0–4–4T no. 30028 propels push-pull set no. 2 away from the Delme viaduct at Fareham on 30 May 1959, substituting for a Hampshire diesel unit on the 10.39 Andover Junction to Portsmouth & Southsea service via Eastleigh. The 93-mile round trip was completed when the 55-year-old Drummond tank reached Andover with the 12.54 from Portsmouth, worked to a diesel schedule. Note the tail lamp alongside the head-code discs on the engine's buffer beam, to cover all eventualities, as the crew would have little time to spare for such niceties if time was to be kept with such an elderly machine.

The exiled Class D1 4–4–0 no. 31735 'on song', sweeping through Fratton non-stop with the 12.15 Portsmouth & Southsea to Plymouth (Friary) through carriages on 10 July 1959. On this duty the engine took the train only as far as Fareham then, after running round and pulling the stock clear, it propelled the Portsmouth portion on to the rear of the Brighton–Plymouth service when that in due course arrived.

The master-plan was to use a curious cross-country train, the 09.27 Southampton Central–Littlehampton, to kick off with steam haulage. However, temptation crossed my path causing a slight deviation from the intended itinerary! Since the winter, Southern Region had been hard put to manage with the Hampshire diesel multiple units and, even when the less intensive service was in force, had been obliged to substitute steam loco-hauled trains occasionally. Mostly, this had been confined to the Andover Junction route (which was closed to all traffic north of Romsey from 7 September 1964) and resulted in a push-pull train being seen at Portsmouth & Southsea (Low Level) on certain Saturdays around lunch-time. The summer timetable had been compiled before this problem became acute, so that some of the scheduled services just could not be met from the available diesel fleet. Thanks to the resourceful Motive Power Superintendent of Eastleigh depot (71A; S. C. Townroe Esq.), the diffi-culties were minimised by reinstating some elderly 4–4–0 locomotives on passenger duties, provided the loads were restricted to four or five coaches only. It was my good fortune on this particular day that the 09.10

Spared the indignity of delay at Portcreek Junction, Class N 2–6–0 no. 31813 gets a clear road on the triangle on Maundy Thursday, 14 April 1960, with the 10.02 through train from Plymouth (Friary) to Portsmouth & Southsea. It was only at such times that Portsmouth had a complete through service all to itself. Note the uncluttered background of Portsdown Hill in those days.

Southampton Central to Portsmouth should be blessed with a former South Eastern & Chatham Class D1 no. 31735. One might have expected to find a rebuilt Wainwright 4–4–0 working between Reading, Guildford and Redhill, or anywhere east thereof, but hardly over the undulating Netley road. Prompt station work, shutting of carriage doors and the shrill note of the guard's whistle ensured minimum delay, then with a staccato exhaust quite unlike the old South Western four-coupled engines 31735 made its exit. Out of the carriage window it was possible to see the locomotive for a few moments as it curved sharply round over the brick arched bridge, then on straight and level track it accelerated away with remarkable spirit – clearly, the crew intended to keep time in a crowded schedule. They were helped by having no intermediate station stops before Fratton, which was just as well if I was to maintain the rest of the day's itinerary! My intended service to Littlehampton was booked to leave Fareham 17 minutes after the train I had boarded, but whereas I was headed for

MONDAY

Portsmouth it would use the avoiding triangle and run direct from Cosham to Havant. Could I get there first? It would all depend on catching a connecting electric train at Fratton.

While awaiting the outcome of such a delicate equation, it was beyond question that 31735 had a fair turn of speed. Before the recent electrification of Kent Coast routes from Victoria and other London terminals to Ramsgate, Deal and Dover such a locomotive might have been called upon to haul relief boat trains or pilot the 'Night Ferry' ahead of a Bulleid Pacific, for which its 6ft. 8in. diameter driving wheels made it entirely suitable. Although, perhaps, something of an unknown quantity on 'Western Section' lines, the refugee made good time to Cosham but application of the brakes heralded adverse signals ahead. The 5-coach train came to a dead stand on the triangle approaching Portcreek Junction, a favourite spot for delays since it marked where the 1848 'branch' met the 1847 'main' line from Havant. Anxious glances at my watch alternated with keeping an eye on the signal ahead – for a couple of minutes it remained obstinately at danger before being hoisted aloft to give us the road. Restarting a passenger train on a curve and slight adverse gradient was not the best opportunity for a large-wheeled 4–4–0 to show its paces, but 31735 managed a creditable effort and cantered along the straight past the gasworks to arrive at Fratton just as the announcer was launching into his litany. 'Bedhampton 'alt, 'avant, Rowlands Castle, Petersfield, Liss, Liphook, 'aslemere, Witley, Milford, Godalming, Farncombe, Guildford (brief pause for breath); Worplesdon, Woking, West Byfleet, West Weybridge, Weybridge, Walton, 'ersham, Esher, Surbiton, then fast to Waterloo.' I leaped out onto the platform, up and over the footbridge, down the other side – steady, steady! – through the barrier and into the comfortable compartment of a 2-BIL electric before collapsing in a towsled heap. One had, as they say, made it.

There were but a few minutes in which to admire the varnished timber and plush cushions of a typical Maunsell carriage before a further change was necessary; this was Havant. The next train in was the aforementioned service from Southampton to Littlehampton, with a Standard 4MT up front. Although having rather smaller driving wheels than the previous steam locomotive, it was a representative example of the free-steaming maids of all work that had proliferated over much of British Railways (and the Southern in particular) during the early 1950s. But since a stopping train to Brighton was booked only 4 minutes behind, the 76xxx 2–6–0 had no time to linger: with familiar rasping sounds from the front end, it scuttled over the junction with the Portsmouth Direct Line from London,

Popular motive power for branch and secondary duties, the Ivatt 2MT 2–6–2T (designed for the LMS) had spread over most of the Southern Region by the sixties. No. 41301 makes a vigorous start from Brighton on 10 June 1961 with an assortment of stock forming a typical Horsham branch train.

and ran non-stop to Chichester ahead of the electric exactly as laid down in the timetable. I changed at Barnham Junction, since my route lay further along the coast as far as Shoreham and would be best accomplished with the following electric train.

Another sprint between platforms was called for at Shoreham, for the local train northwards up the Adur estuary had already arrived from Brighton. It consisted of an elderly pair of push-pull coaches of South Eastern & Chatham origin, like the H Class locomotive no. 31308 coupled on at the front. Though not indigenous to the Brighton area, once the native D1 0–4–2T and D3 0–4–4T designs had gone the Wainwright H tanks were generally preferred to Drummond M7s on 'motor-train' working hereabouts; doubtless such sentiments were reversed at depots like Bournemouth, Eastleigh or Fratton! The weather was overcast, unfortunately, but on a fine day the train ride up through the South Downs must have been very beautiful. Despite quite frequent stops at country

Christ's Hospital (West Horsham) station on 24 April 1960. In the Down main platform is one of the newly-converted push-pull sets, 604, created from surplus 1930s Maunsell corridor carriages, strengthened by a former SECR ten-compartment non-corridor all-third. While, at first glance, the Horsham–Brighton train bears some similarity to a Hampshire DMU, at the rear a faithful Drummond M7 0–4–4T (no. 30051) provides the oomph!

stations – there was only half a mile between Bramber and Steyning – the 20-mile journey to Horsham took less than fifty minutes, including replenishment of 31308's water supply en route. I was a little surprised to discover the branch was double-track throughout and, indeed, that this steam-operated line provided an hourly service in either direction; very different from 'The Middy' of my schooldays. Yet in March 1966 this useful route was closed and ripped up under the Beeching regime, which was a real paradox in the light of Southern Railway plans to electrify it.

Shortly after leaving Southwater station, the train approached Itching-field Junction, not in itself a station but the northern apex of a triangle of routes whose base was the coastal line from Chichester to Brighton. Back on third-rail track, in no time 31308 drew up at Christ's Hospital (West Horsham). If the timetable had been planned with cross-country journeys in mind, a similar motor-train might have been waiting in the adjoining platform to provide connections for Cranleigh and Guildford – perhaps I

With stencil headcode 'I' exhibited, elderly 4-SUB electric unit 4329 stands in the deep shadows cast by the vast structure of Waterloo station on 6 February 1961, before leaving Platform 2 for Horsham via Motspur Park.

Synonymous with Brighton line electrification, two 4-LAV units (with 2928 leading) approach Merstham on a Down stopping service on 5 March 1967. Apart from the yellow warning panel painted on each end of the set and the horns mounted on the roof, these 1933-built EMUs remained virtually unaltered throughout their existence.

Still practically new, Bo-Bo electric locomotive E5003 powers through Three Bridges with Boat Train stock from Newhaven to London (Victoria) on 10 August 1959. This proved to be the author's first sighting of one of these unusual locomotives, which featured the Southern's bogie-mounted third-rail pick-up shoes and a central pantograph as well.

could travel that line tomorrow? Most connections had to be made at the main Horsham station, a couple of miles further on, although there proved to be precious little time to spare upon arrival. Doors were being closed on one of the older varieties of 4-SUB electric multiple units alongside, making ready to depart for Crawley, Three Bridges and the main Brighton line to Victoria. At off-peak times such as this, one could enjoy reasonable comfort in a non-corridor train, but in the rush hour it was a case of every sardine for him- (or her-) self!

Calling at all intermediate stations and halts to Crawley, there were still signs of the quieter past before this whole area became a New Town boom district, swallowed up in the development of Gatwick airport. As the track curved round to the left, there was a glimpse of smoke and steam at Three Bridges shed (75E) in the narrowing angle formed by the Brighton main line before the electric swung round into the platform – time to get off. On the opposite side of the station was a small bay platform with trainshed for cross-country services to East Grinstead. Empty and draughty on a grey

Chatham engine, Brighton carriages. The East Grinstead shuttle on 10 August 1959 consisted of Class H 0–4–4T (no. 31162) and push-pull set no. 650, still in Carmine livery. The brick-built trainshed for the bay can be seen behind the carriages. Sadly, this useful cross-country route was closed from 2 January 1967.

day such as this, one was left to contemplate activities on the main line for a while: there were still plenty of electric trains from the earliest days of Sir Herbert Walker's 'brave new world' begun in 1932, with 4-LAV units on stopping services and 6-PUL or 6-PAN sets on the faster schedules. The famous 5-BEL Pullman sets comprising the 'Brighton Belle' were still painted in their traditional umber and cream livery in 1959, though none passed through while I waited; their demise did not come until 1972. But I was rewarded by one of the new Bo-Bo electric locomotives, E5003, swishing through with an Up Newhaven Boat Express. With its pantograph and third rail pick-ups, its wedge shape seemed strange even to those accustomed to the unconventional Bulleid designs. The contrast was especially marked when the motor-train for East Grinstead arrived. Seen from the platform, one's first impression was of a pre-Grouping electric set, since it was being propelled from the rear. The carriages were of pure LBSCR origin, complete with layers of timber panelling, even if it was painted in the all-over carmine associated with early BR non-corridor stock. Set no. 650 was a perfect museum piece of pre-First World War vintage, being operated by yet another heirloom from the SECR, Class H 0–4–4T no. 31162.

Having got rather cold standing on the platform, I was glad to get inside the leading compartment. However, any hopes of much warmth within were confounded when daylight was identified around the doorway! Nevertheless, this little train provided an hourly connection for residents at Rowfant and Grange Road, two charming country stations with level crossings set amid trees and rhododendrons, as well as linking East Grinstead with the main Brighton line. Having called at West Grinstead earlier in the day, I was interested to see what East Grinstead looked like.

With its dome glinting in the winter sunshine, Class H 0–4–4T no. 31278 makes a spirited departure from Rowfant with an afternoon motor-train to Three Bridges on 14 March 1962. Only the converted Maunsell push-pull carriages betray any evidence of modernisation.

A 1964 view of the Low Level platforms at East Grinstead, with the High Level in the background. Following the success of the Hampshire diesel-electric multiple unit pilot scheme, begun in 1957, a modified design for the East Sussex network of non-electrified routes was built in 1962. Three-car set no. 1315 has terminated in the Down platform (where trains formerly ran through to Horsted Keynes and Lewes) prior to making a return trip to Oxted.

Thanks to the loan of a pre-war 'Coronet' folding camera, the author was able to obtain this souvenir of Riddles' Standard 4MT 2–6–4T no. 80031 at Brighton – where it was built – on 22 April 1954. These locomotives were to form the backbone of cross-country operations, particularly in East Sussex.

MONDAY

In the quarter of an hour available to me between connections, I discovered a split-level station: the upper handled cross-country traffic between Three Bridges and Tunbridge Wells, while the lower served merely as a terminal for some services from East Croydon and Oxted, since closure the previous year of the route southwards to Horsted Keynes and Lewes (the Bluebell line). Nor had the Horsted Keynes–Sheffield Park section yet been reopened under private ownership, for the idea of individual (as opposed to BR) interests buying, stocking and operating a standard gauge line was still very radical at this period. A distant whistle reminded me that I had another train to catch, so I hurriedly made my way back to the upper level to travel behind one of the Standard 4MT 2–6–4T engines built at Brighton Works in the mid-1950s.

With the station buildings perched on the roadside, above the tracks, Class N 2–6–0 no. 31411 gruffly announces its departure from Eridge with an Eastbourne–Tunbridge Wells West service via the 'Cuckoo Line'. A Standard 4MT 2–6–4T waits in the siding with empty stock, to provide a connection for Oxted via Ashurst and Edenbridge (Town).

On a dull summer afternoon, Wainwright Class H 0–4–4T no. 31544 bustles away from Tunbridge Wells West station with a motor-train bound for Oxted on 10 August 1959. The unique 'Q' 0–6–0 with stove-pipe chimney (30549) simmers outside the shed. The Oxted push-pull set is a strange combination: a Chatham ten-compartment all-third has been married to a Brighton driving trailer/brake (S3823S), without an official 'set number'.

Repton (Class V 4–4–0 no. 30926) hurtles through Tonbridge station on 10 August 1959 with the Up 'Man of Kent' express, the three-cylinder exhaust merging into one continuous roar. This locomotive survives in exile in North America.

The slab-sided contours of push-pull set 482 indicate its SECR origins, each carriage having been converted from an Edwardian steam rail-motor. Painted in BR Carmine livery, this set was being propelled by 'H' tank 31319 near Brasted Halt on Sunday, 12 July 1959, towards Dunton Green. These quaint survivors could be found working on the Westerham branch until 1960, which itself closed to all traffic from 30 October 1961.

The stock comprised a four-coach set of Maunsell 'slim-line' corridor coaches suitable for the restricted clearances of certain tunnels in Kent and East Sussex. Having originated at London's Victoria station and travelled via Oxted, the remaining 13½ miles to Tunbridge Wells West would be child's play to the husky tank, a worthy successor to Earle Marsh's I3 4–4–2T design dating from the Edwardian era. With the sharp exhaust characteristic of Riddles' Standard locomotives, no. 80152 set off eastward with long loping strides, called at Forest Row, Hartfield and Withyham along the upper reaches of the River Medway before meeting the direct route from Oxted again at the approach to Groombridge. The line from Eridge also merged at this point, itself the junction for Lewes (via Uckfield) and the 'Cuckoo Line' from Eastbourne. So many of these useful cross-country routes were to be truncated or abandoned in the next decade that much of the reasoning behind their construction was lost,

25

At 4 p.m. on weekdays the Down Main platform at Tonbridge was occupied by two local trains buffered up one behind the other. 4MT 2–6–4T no. 80019 was heading the 16.10 to Tunbridge Wells and Eastbourne (via Eridge) on 10 August 1959, while Ivatt 2MT 2–6–2T 41310 had charge of the 16.12 to Margate via Ashford service.

The charming little branch terminus at Hawkhurst on 10 August 1959. 'H' tank no. 31193 and Carmine-liveried motor-set 652 provide a perfect 'period' train as they wait to return to Paddock Wood with the 17.00 service.

resulting in yet more closures as their lifeblood ebbed away. From Groombridge we ran non-stop, passing the site of the closed halt at High Rocks – a notable beauty spot – before running into the impressive Tunbridge Wells West station, not far from the Pantiles. There stood a traditional brick-built engine shed beside the arrival platform, a temptation if ever there was one, but in order to reach Hawkhurst (and get home) that day, the schedule must be adhered to. A connection for Tunbridge Wells Central, High Brooms and Tonbridge waited impatiently to negotiate the tight bore of the tunnel ahead, with another 4MT tank (80146) in charge, then it was off.

Electrification had not yet come upon Tonbridge. It was still possible to watch a 'Schools' Class 4–4–0 hurtle through with the Up 'Man of Kent',

While the Strood–Maidstone (West) line had been electrified before World War II, the section thence via Wateringbury to Paddock Wood remained a steam-operated backwater until 1961, some trains continuing along the main line to and from Tonbridge. In this scene at Maidstone (West), a familiar Wainwright tank engine (31512) heads a local service from Paddock Wood into one of the 'electrified' platforms in order to detach the ex-LMS 'fitted' van coupled between it and the carriages. It will then be able to resume normal push-pull working for the return journey and use its own special platform (seen on the far right, behind the white fence).

One of the more interesting cross-country services that formerly reversed (and changed engines) at Redhill ran between Margate and Birkenhead. On 27 December 1958 the three carriages from Margate continue their long journey to Merseyside behind 4MT 2–6–0 no. 76059 as it barks away from Redhill's Platform 2, the route being via Guildford and Reading (General).

or a Boat Train for the Channel ports set all the rubbish dancing in the wake of a Bulleid Pacific 'on song'. Quaint push-pull sets formed from erstwhile SECR steam railmotors worked out to Dunton Green and Westerham, while in due course the Down main platform found itself host to two local trains, one behind the other. As soon as the Tunbridge Wells and Eastbourne service had blasted away behind yet another ubiquitous 2–6–4T, a stopping train for Margate whistled its impending departure. I climbed aboard for just the short trip to Paddock Wood, but it seemed remarkable that a small engine like a 'Mickey Mouse' Class 2MT 2–6–2T should be entrusted with the lengthy journey out to the East Kent coast. No. 41310 bustled along in lively fashion and soon deposited me at the junction for the Hop-pickers' line. The Hawkhurst bay was on the Up side, so it was necessary to cross over by the long footbridge and await the next branch train. When it arrived, I was pleased to find it was entirely in keeping with the very rural nature of this 11½-mile line – another elderly H tank coupled to a former LBSCR 'motor-train' set 652. After courteous enquiry as to one's destination, carriage doors were closed and the little train set off into the Weald of Kent.

The journey took thirty minutes, with intermediate pauses at Hors-

MONDAY

monden, Goudhurst and Cranbrook. Travellers had time to appreciate the distinctive oast-houses from the carriage windows, while near Hors-monden the single track was noticeably grass-grown in a dank cutting; it was a very pastoral scene. At the terminus one had just a few minutes to snatch a photograph of the branch train in its rustic environment before departure, for one engine in steam was the only economic way to operate such a line. Even so, within two years it would be closed completely, another victim of the harsh reality of rationalisation, yet one more loss to the traditional fabric of country life. But, as a railway enthusiast, one was

A relic of inter-Regional co-operation could be unearthed in the use of a Western locomotive in each direction between Reading and Redhill on weekdays, to familiarise the crews with 'foreign' engines in case of emergency or diversions. Nothing larger than a 'Blue' engine was permitted by the Southern, so the usual motive power for this operation was a 2–6–0 or 'Manor' 4–6–0. On 10 January 1962 'Mogul' 6379 makes a majestic exit from Gomshall & Shere with a Redhill to Reading service, while the platform shelter, gas lamp and milk churns create a timeless image.

learning to savour each moment while it lasted. Once boasting a polished brass dome and intricate livery, but now painted in simple black with red and grey lining, Wainwright 0–4–4T no. 31193 was put into reverse gear and, with its driver directing activities from the end compartment of the push-pull trailer, the whole soothing process was repeated in the direction of Paddock Wood. Though I managed to be present when the line closed in July 1961, this was to be my only journey over the Hawkhurst branch and I found it captivating.

Hardly had I stepped down on to the platform at Paddock Wood when another push-pull train drew alongside, forming a Maidstone West to Tonbridge service. Although providing me with a fourth H tank (31319) that day, the two-coach set no. 732 was a LSWR corridor survivor of a kind remembered from the Midhurst branch. Just fancy bowling along one of the fastest stretches of main line in Kent, travelling in an expatriate South Western train coupled to a former Chatham engine, the whole outfit being at least fifty years old! Tonbridge was reached in all the excitement of the rush hour, which effectively precluded any more photography. Nevertheless, again there was a good connection, for Redhill and Guildford this time, and yet another new experience with motive power. At home in Fareham it was not at all unusual to find Maunsell 2–6–0 'Moguls' at work on both passenger and goods trains, almost always two-cylinder examples of Class U or N, turn and turn about with the Standard 4MT locomotives; but in Kent the three-cylinder variants (Classes U1 or N1) were to be found on similar tasks. The difference was that, whilst there were eighty two-cylinder N Class engines, there were just six of the N1 – and no. 31879 of the latter was in charge from Tonbridge to Redhill. Apart from a more 'mushy' exhaust note, one was not conscious of any great difference in performance. Reversal was necessary at Redhill, but the carriages continued on to Guildford and, ultimately, to Reading (South). I changed at Guildford, making my way home via the Portsmouth Direct line in the company of an attractive young lady who needed guidance on how to reach – of all places – Fareham. That was a bonus not advertised in the Rail Rover leaflet!

TUESDAY

'DIRECT' FROM PORTSMOUTH TO SURREY AND SUSSEX

The glimpse of the Guildford–Horsham branch the previous day was enough to prompt further investigation in that area. As it had been getting dark on the way home from Guildford the night before, it seemed a good idea to travel that way again in daylight. An earlier train from Fareham – which originated at Eastleigh – provided a run to Portsmouth with a steam locomotive of a different type altogether. Perhaps because its engines had been allowed a slightly more generous loading gauge than those of its neighbours, the tender locomotives built by the London, Brighton & South Coast Railway were generally somewhat restricted after the Grouping into the Southern Railway in 1923. During the early years of British Railways, the only survivors of the 'Brighton' were a handful of B4 and rebuilt B4x 4–4–0s, nearly all in store, two varieties of 4–4–2 Atlantics (Classes H1 and H2), seventeen 'Moguls' of Class K and an assortment of 0–6–0 goods engines of Classes C2, C2x and C3. True, there were also seven 'Remembrance' 4–6–0s, but they had been rebuilt from 4–6–4T locomotives by the Southern Railway following electrification of the Brighton main line, and naturally conformed to the more restricted dimensions thereafter. By 1959 all but the K class 2–6–0s and some C2x 'Vulcans' had gone, and they were used mostly on freight. However, a pair of the former were shedded first at Fratton and then Eastleigh for most of the fifties, the appointed engines being 32337 and 32349. Because of the position with the diesel multiple units, both found themselves drafted in for passenger duties

Pressed into passenger service for the summer season, one of the pair of 'K' 2–6–0s based at Eastleigh (71A) clips along at a smart pace with the 18.33 Portsmouth & Southsea to Southampton Central train on 31 July 1959. No. 32349 has just passed beneath Highlands Road bridge to the west of Fareham, a route not normally worked by the Brighton 'Moguls' – next stop, Netley.

Between Havant and Guildford, the Portsmouth Direct line twists and turns amid lovely countryside. Wonderful vistas open up for the passenger looking out of the carriage window. When this scenic route was the preserve of the 4-COR 'Nelson' units, the only word of advice was to hang on tight! In this sixties view, green-liveried 4-COR carriages head south near Peasmarsh Junction with an early evening express from London (Waterloo) to Portsmouth Harbour.

during the height of the summer season. As luck would have it, 32337 headed the train to Portsmouth, which must have been a much lighter load than the 10.03 Eastleigh–Fratton goods or the heavier Salisbury to Chichester freight, normally the province of such engines.

At Portsmouth & Southsea I left the 'Mogul' in the Low Level terminus before making my way up the staircase to the High Level for a fast train to Guildford. Normally one would change trains at Fratton, but fast services for Waterloo did not stop there. All regular operations via the Portsmouth Direct line throughout the day fell into a neat pattern of half-hourly slow and hourly fast trains, the latter being provided by Maunsell corridor four-coach sets built for the electrification of this route in 1937. These were generally marshalled into rakes of eight or twelve cars, one set

Despite electrification of the passenger trains, freight remained steam-hauled almost to the last. On 25 October 1958 Bulleid Q1 0–6–0 no. 33002 bustles along with a trainload of vans between Petersfield and Rowlands Castle, due at 10.40. This had originated as the 04.50 pick-up goods from Woking Down Yard, 33002 being shedded at Guildford (70C).

having refreshment facilities. Whilst there were some sub-classes (such as 4-BUF, 4-RES etc.), the entire group was commonly known as 4-COR or 'Nelson' sets, the most likely reason for this nickname being their long association with Portsmouth. While Nelson's *Victory* remains preserved inside the dockyard, within walking distance of Portsmouth Harbour station, there may be another reason. Alone amongst Maunsell's designs for electric multiple units in having corridor connections between sets, the route indicator stencils of 4-COR units had to be positioned on the opposite side of the cab to the driver's window with the corridor connection mounted between; this gave them an odd 'one-eyed' demeanour and a unique character. Anyone who has ever stood on the platform

Looking commendably clean, Class D1 4–4–0 no. 31247 clears its tubes before leaving Platform 5 at Guildford with the 09.03 Reading (South) to Redhill service on 14 September 1957. These successful engines were created by Maunsell from rebuilding Wainwright's 'Coppertops' during the last years of the South Eastern & Chatham Railway. A similar programme had been put in hand with the smaller-wheeled 'E' class, and both types of rebuild survived into the 1960s on local and semi-fast duties.

TUESDAY

---

of a wayside station when a train of 4-COR units was approaching at speed, corridor connections swaying in syncopated rhythm, will know just what I mean! It is fortunate that one complete set was acquired for perservation when the 4-COR type was finally retired in 1972.

If the older electric sets had a fault, it could only be their liability to oscillate at speed, particularly when the third rail changed sides. After the Havant stop (not observed throughout the day), speed rose rapidly on the straight track to Rowlands Castle in spite of an almost unrelenting adverse gradient: it was just this sort of ability that revolutionised the Portsmouth Direct line on electrification. As the train approached the tunnel at Buriton, power was eased for the permanent restrictions through the

Although much of their time was spent on cross-London freight duties, the rugged Class H16 4–6–2T locomotives designed by Urie might sometimes be found further afield. On 23 November 1957, 30518 nearly succeeded in eluding the camera as it reversed past the turntable at Guildford, before disappearing in the direction of Woking and its home shed of Feltham (70B).

---

reverse curves; once over the top and through the black hole under the Downs, speed rose again dramatically and Petersfield was passed at a thundering 70m.p.h. In a matter of minutes Liss flashed by, with a momentary image of the Longmoor Military Railway station and exchange sidings if one knew where to look. The 1 in 80 gradient of Liss Bank took its toll and, after a relatively level mile or two either side of Liphook, the incline steepened again to 1 in 100 to the summit at Haslemere. No serious attempt was made to discontinue freight traffic over the Portsmouth Direct line yet, for coal yards remained in use at all the main stations until 1966, although the daily freight was reduced to a MWFO operation as an economy measure. Almost immediately after restarting, it

Difficult to photograph against the low winter sunlight, Guildford's shed pilot engine on 23 November 1957 was 30086. Designed by Adams and built in 1891 for use on the sharply-curved sidings within Southampton Docks, this 'B4' 0–4–0T was formerly named *Havre*. Note the lumps of coal perched on the tank-top and boiler and the half-roundhouse layout.

TUESDAY

was downhill at 1 in 80 practically to Witley where, after a momentary check, the line continued in headlong descent past the Milford lakes to Godalming. Sweeping through the reverse curves, first on an embankment then in a cutting, the Portsmouth Direct extension of 1859 linked up with the original 1849 route and continued northwards through two tunnels to Guildford. In passing, there were two junctions as other tracks came in from the east, but I'll return to them in a little while. The Waterloo express came to a stand in platforms 6 and 7, setting down passengers for Aldershot, Farnborough and Reading as well as those heading east for Redhill; Guildford had been one of those select stations where, before the Grouping, examples of all three main constituent companies of the Southern Railway used to meet.

With shed and tunnel as a background, Drummond Class M7 0–4–4T no. 30047 coasts into Guildford station with the 09.30 motor train from Horsham on 21 October 1958. To obtain this picture, the photographer had to point the camera under the Farnham Road overbridge and hope for the best!

RAIL ROVER

Although sharp-eyed passengers who knew where to look could get a glimpse of Guildford shed (70C) and its occupants as Up trains slid out of the second of the two tunnels, an hour or two on the platforms could be much more rewarding. Equally, it could be very frustrating if a particular engine remained hidden in the roundhouse. On occasions I managed to persuade the foreman to let me visit the shed, but even then frustrations could persist for it was a fiendish place for photography. Because of its location immediately to the north of the tunnel, it was likely to be either in shadow or against the light, while inside the shed it could be as black as

Definitely a period piece! Relegated to branch line and spare duties, the Saturdays-only service between Guildford and Cranleigh provided an outing for one of the old South Eastern & Chatham non-corridor 'Birdcage' sets on 23 November 1957, while Class E4 'Radial' 0–6–2T no. 32506 made a spirited start for the tunnel at the south end of Guildford station. Within weeks this classic combination on the 13.09 service to Cranleigh had ceased, for the elderly, panelled three-coach sets with their distinctive guard's look-out had been withdrawn.

Although the goods ran only three days a week, it was always worth seeing. With the rest of its train left on the running line, Class M7 0–4–4T no. 30132 prepares to shunt a van into the Fuller's Earth Works siding at Baynards on St Valentine's Day, 1962. Note the timber loading gauge in the yard and the unfitted goods wagons. The entire picture has a nineteenth-century flavour.

The 09.22 Guildford to Horsham service curves away from the Portsmouth Direct main line at Peasmarsh Junction behind 'Mickey Mouse' 2MT 2–6–2T no. 41260 on 1 November 1961. Passengers on the branch that morning were being treated to rather superior stock, which consisted of a three-coach Standard Mk. I set (no. 539), though the mainly commuter traffic to and from London was not enough to save the line.

The lovely little station at Baynards provides the setting for 2MT 2–6–2T no. 41260 with the 10.34 Guildford–Horsham branch train on 24 November 1961. The three-coach train on this occasion is one of the Bulleid 'Shorties' with doors to every compartment.

pitch. Some locomotives seemed to linger up by the coaling stage, while others might come as far as the turntable before running back to the yard or away to Woking, light engine. Although no Bulleid Pacifics were shedded at Guildford, it was not unusual to see one by the coaling stage between duties. A small engine was needed as shed pilot, since it was required to clear the ash from the pits and turn the wagon (coupled to itself) on the turntable before propelling it up to the yard for disposal. For years this had been the province of a former Southampton Docks 0–4–0ST, no. 30458 *Ironside*, but after its withdrawal in the mid-1950s the usual incumbent was a Class B4 0–4–0T.

Straddling the two counties of Surrey and West Sussex as it did, the Guildford to Horsham branch line was another of those useful cross-country routes that fulfilled a dual function. Not only did it provide a valuable social service between the villages and small towns along its

41

Christ's Hospital branch platforms (the main platforms for the Brighton and Mid-Sussex lines were behind the hedge on the right of the picture). Note the very short signal post, ground-frame and twin platform faces for the Guildford trains. This last feature can still be found at Horsted Keynes on the former LBSCR Bluebell Railway.

route, but for the traveller who was not in a hurry it also offered a relaxing and congestion-free means of getting to the coast. As was noted 'yesterday', at Horsham the branch fed into a further complex of cross-country lines which could take the traveller eastward into Kent. Had the Rail Rover ticket been available in, say, 1954 it would have been possible to indulge in a circular tour via Pulborough, Midhurst and Petersfield. Nevertheless, its potential was not lost on the Southern, who periodically arranged excursions on Sundays that traversed both the Guildford–Horsham and Horsham–Shoreham branches as a means of getting to Brighton. Such trains were worked by tender locomotives, usually 0–6–0s of either C2x, Q or Q1 classes, which had adequate power as well as supplies of fuel and water to complete the journey, for there were severe limits on the size and weight of engines permitted between Peasmarsh Junction and Christ's Hospital. For normal daily operations tank engines

Coaling by rail-mounted crane at Horsham (75D) depot. One of the curious double-domed 0–6–0 tender engines of Class C2x, 32527, was receiving attention on 29 June 1959 while an auto-fitted 'H' 0–4–4T (31543) waited its turn by the water column. Forty-five of the C2 class were rebuilt with larger C3-type boilers from 1908 onwards and the final examples lasted until 1962; what a pity one was not preserved.

were provided for both passenger and freight, although the latter had certain peculiarities, as will be seen.

Until February 1955, Guildford shed had been responsible for supplying some locomotives for the Alton–Fareham (Meon Valley), Petersfield–Midhurst and Bentley–Bordon branches in addition to the Horsham line; all required push-pull engines of Class M7. Thereafter only the Horsham and Bordon branches remained open to passenger traffic, and the allocation was accordingly reduced. When Bordon lost its passenger trains in September 1957, fewer still were needed. Most push-pull M7s were transferred away from Guildford: some to Bournemouth, others to former 'Brighton' depots in Sussex and Kent (where they were not always very welcome!). The vacuum was filled in part by an influx of newish 2MT 2–6–2Ts designed by Ivatt originally for the LMS,

Occasional shortages of push-pull fitted locomotives created extra work for crews and signalmen. A stalwart at Horsham depot for many years, Class E4 0–6–2T no. 32469 substitutes for an 'H' or 'M7' on the 15.09 Horsham–Guildford branch train on 29 June 1959. Galloping along in fine style, 32469 does not look out of place with ex-SECR push-pull set no. 663, although the nearly empty coal bunker may indicate that the E4 was switched on to the Guildford service at the last minute. The picture was taken between Christ's Hospital and Slinfold, when the 'Radial' still had about 16 miles to go!

but which continued under British Railways more or less as a standard class; many spent their entire working lives on the Southern. Thus, the Horsham branch was worked by both 'motor-trains' and ordinary locomotives pulling an assortment of stock, ranging from push-pull sets to early Bulleid corridor carriages. Guildford was not entirely bereft of M7s, but almost all those remaining were not auto-fitted and were used for shunting or light goods work. For the most part then, any push-pull trains tended to be provided by Horsham depot (75D), but the freight was handled by Guildford which frequently turned out an M7 0–4–4T, at least on Wednesdays and Fridays. Mondays, it seems, were different. For some obscure reason, the 0–6–0 diesel shunter at Horsham was provided by Guildford and, once a week, the opportunity was taken to change over the locomotive by employing it on the branch goods. This being a Tuesday, however, no goods would be running at all.

Rush hour at Cranleigh: Brighton-based 'H' 0–4–4T no. 31276 is coupled at the rear of push-pull set 605 for Horsham while Drummond 'M7' 30110 prepares to propel set 601 towards Guildford. This busy scene on 4 July 1960 encapsulates the evening peak on a rural branch line before the Beeching era swept it all away.

If one missed the 10.34 from Guildford, there was a three-hour wait for the next. Whatever the Ivatt 2–6–2Ts lacked in vintage appeal, they had a certain style all their own. They were not nicknamed 'Mickey Mouse' tanks for nothing! It was fascinating to ride behind one through the tunnels, and hear a cheerful chuckling from the front end, even if it was wise to shut the carriage windows to keep out swirling, sulphurous fumes. Soon after emerging into daylight could be seen the signals for Shalford Junction, the route taken by my train from Redhill the previous evening. For the moment, the little tank engine kept ahead on the electrified tracks towards Portsmouth, but at the next junction it slowed to collect the single line tablet from the Peasmarsh signalman. Curving sharply to the left, it soon passed beneath a narrow girder bridge and shuffled along beside the stump of the Wey & Arun canal to the first station at Bramley & Wonersh. Besides having a busy level crossing, it was

RAIL ROVER

also a passing place at certain times of the day, with a fair amount of commuter traffic. In fact, the station was very well positioned and, if taken on its own, was likely to be profitable. After restarting, the train kept company with the A281 road for about a mile before drifting away eastward close to the course of the old canal at Run Common. Finally, canal and railway went their separate ways as Cranleigh was approached.

Although on the outskirts of the town, Cranleigh was the most important station on the line and was responsible for much of its traffic, both passenger and goods. On Saturdays only, an additional service was run from Guildford to Cranleigh at lunchtime; just the task for a 'Brighton' E4 0–6–2T and three-coach 'Birdcage' set in days gone by, as I recall. Had this been a Monday, Wednesday or Friday, the goods train would have been shunting in the yard during the morning, too. Instead, the 'Mickey Mouse' had no cause to stay and chattered over the minor level crossing at the east of the station before heading away into the country towards Baynard's Park. The countryside on the Surrey/Sussex border was quite charming, the only hint of industry being the Fullers Earth works hidden in the trees just before Baynards station. It had its own private siding, occasionally requiring wagons to be shunted in or out. As at both previous stations, passing facilities were available at Baynards but seemed to be needed only in connection with the Up goods.

Shortly after leaving this picturesque spot, the train passed beneath a skew bridge and then plunged into a tunnel; when it emerged, it was in Sussex. Almost immediately, the brakes were on for the single platform at Rudgwick. The station was in fact much nearer to Bucks Green, but no doubt modern infilling has brought the two closer since the railway closed in June 1965. An odd feature of the layout was the way in which the line to Slinfold curved away, while straight ahead was the headshunt for the cramped goods yard. Although not elevated to the position of a passing station, Rudgwick still qualified as a block-post with full signalling. Not far ahead, the line crossed the A281 road; the bridge at this point was for years a constraint upon operators of both lorries and buses, since the height of vehicles was restricted to single-deckers. First on an embankment, then in a cutting, the branch meandered south-eastwards to dive beneath the main A29 road just before Slinfold, another non-passing station rated as a block-post. The single track unfolded straight and true for more than a mile before curving beneath the A264 road (to Broadbridge Heath), the final station being at Christ's Hospital, where it had two platforms all to itself, 17¼ miles from Guildford.

On arrival at Horsham once more, there was time to explore. The motive power depot was several hundred yards away along the road, but well worth the effort. It must have been my lucky day, for I was allowed to visit the shed; as at Guildford, it was grouped round the turntable in the form of a roundhouse. I was some years too late for either the E5 or E5x 0–6–2T locos, which were sometimes used on the goods train to Midhurst and Petersfield in the early 1950s, but one or two of the large 'Vulcan' C2x 0–6–0s were to be seen, including an example with the curious double-domed boiler. When the last D3 0–4–4T had retired from push-pull duties on the Guildford to Horsham line (no. 32390), H tanks filled the breach

The best view of Guildford shed (if one was unable to visit it) could be obtained from passing trains. This vantage point produced an endearing study of elderly 'South Western' motive power on 7 February 1962, with Adams 'B4' 0–4–0T 30089 chimney-to-chimney with 'M7' 0–4–4T no. 30049. For an unsolicited comment on the changing fortunes of Britain's railways, one need look no further than the chalked graffiti on the water column: 'Dr Beeching's 3% special'.

quite adequately. Also to be found were a few of the smaller-wheeled E4 'Radials', which took turns on the Midhurst goods with the C2x 0–6–0s. They were also used, occasionally, as substitutes on passenger duties; no. 32469 in particular fulfilled this role over the years, for I can remember it once running bunker-first with a push-pull set, replacing a failed M7 on 'The Middy'. Not being equipped for that sort of operation, the crew had no option but to run round at each terminal, which might not be too much of a problem at Guildford (where there were eight platform faces) but certainly caused some disruption at Petersfield.

I will not bore the reader with a detailed description of the return journey, since it retraced exactly the routes already given. Since closure, much of the trackbed has gone back to nature while part has been utilized for road improvement. Commuters still travel to London each weekday, but most take their cars to either Guildford or Horsham where rush-hour congestion has defied all attempts at solution. Compared with the swarm of vehicles and their attendant pollution, Dr Beeching's cure for an unprofitable railway today seems singularly inappropriate. *Sic transit Gloria mundi.*

THE MIDHURST GOODS, THEN BY 'GREYHOUND' TO GREYFRIARS

One of the things I specially wanted to do during the Rail Rover week was visit some of the less accessible railway lines or those where the passenger services had been 'suspended', even if this meant supplementing rail travel with some mileage on two wheels. How else could one keep tabs on Lavant, or Midhurst?

Apart from during the sugar beet season, the Lavant goods was rather difficult to predict. When passenger traffic between Chichester and Midhurst was withdrawn in July 1935, goods trains continued to serve the intermediate stations of Lavant, Singleton and Cocking. This situation persisted into the early years of Nationalisation, but heavy rains washed away a culvert north of Cocking and caused the derailment of a C2x 'Vulcan' with the northbound goods on the morning of 19 November 1951. Although the engine, no. 32522, was eventually recovered from the stream and repaired at Brighton Works, through freight traffic was abandoned and activities restricted to the Chichester–Lavant section only after 26 August 1953. Even though Lavant itself closed on 3 August 1968, most of the remaining stump has been retained in connection with gravel workings nearby. In the Introduction I explained that passenger services over the other lines to Midhurst had been withdrawn on 5 February 1955, but freight continued to be handled over the branch from Pulborough; between Petersfield and Midhurst Common the former London & South Western branch line (opened on 1 September 1864) was closed in its entirety.

This classic Victorian station of 1881 retained its dignity even after closure, for Midhurst was not forgotton. A Ramblers' excursion from Charing Cross via Epsom reached the West Sussex town on Sunday, 8 June 1958, the first passenger train since 6 February 1955, hauled by the unique stovepipe-chimney Class Q 0–6–0 no. 30549. The load was eight former LSWR 'Ironclad' corridor coaches (set 442). In this picture the Maunsell locomotive was running round its carriages before departing again eastwards with the empty stock. Former LBSCR features still abound, for only the signal arms had been removed in the intervening three years.

On Wednesday, 12 August 1959, I made the pilgrimage to Midhurst by road. It wasn't the first visit since leaving school, because there had been a Ramblers' Excursion on Sunday, 8 June 1958, which even imminent examinations had been unable to keep me from. But as the amount of freight was seldom sufficient to warrant running a train every weekday, the usual pattern became MWFO. This was discovered the hard way, i.e. by turning up on a Tuesday and finding no train! Thereafter, as a precaution, I telephoned the goods depot before setting out – no train, no trip. But this particular day all was well: the locomotive might be tender-first, cross winds could blow smoke all over everything or the skies might open in a deluge, but at least it would run. Much less certain was the time it would run. I have stood, sat and grown old by the lineside, camera at the ready, waiting for trains that were guaranteed to run. Setting

Double-domed 'C2x' 0–6–0 no. 32527 is framed in the western portal of the tunnel at Midhurst during shunting on 12 August 1959. The headcode disc appears to be in the wrong position, but on such a rural duty this was of no particular significance. It is believed the crew were Messrs Lambert and Brooks of Horsham depot.

aside both Murphy's Law and miracles, all the photographer of freight trains needs is a little luck. Whatever was needed, it was my good fortune to find C2x 0–6–0 no. 32527 shunting Midhurst yard and be invited to share some cold tea with the crew. Later, I scootered along the A286 road a short distance and turned off on a narrow lane to Ambersham until it crossed over the single line, just east of the tunnel. From the overbridge there was an excellent view of the railway, so I sat on the mossy stonework and prepared to wait. After a little, one's ears began to play tricks, mistaking the sighing of the wind in the trees for a train approaching. At last it was beyond doubt: a shrill quavering whistle carried through the murky tunnel, then the distinctive hollow 'chaff, chaff' of a 'Vulcan' on the move as it progressed cautiously through the narrow bore. The sound became louder, though as yet there were no tell-tale wisps of steam from the tunnel mouth to confirm the train was coming. First into view came the engine's tender, then for a moment the rest of the train was obscured by pent-up steam and smoke as it emerged into daylight. While the crew waved a cheery greeting, the Midhurst goods plodded steadily on into the dense woodland of Cowdray Park. A moment to savour, to remember and to re-live long after it had gone out of sight, vanished into the mists of the Victorian Age in which such a railway had been kindled. If the reader should go for a walk today along that country lane and linger for a while by the mossy bridge, it may not be too easy to summon up the spirits of a long-departed railway. Vigorous young saplings now grow in the cutting between the tunnel mouth and the bridge while, on the other side, spoil has been levelled until any vestige of a railway – extended from

From a vantage point in the 'V' formed by the junction of the Petersfield and Chichester branches at Midhurst, the author was able to obtain his first picture of the goods since passenger traffic had ceased in 1955. 'Vulcan' C2x 0–6–0 no. 32522 shuffles past some wagons whilst running round on 11 June 1958, the original LSWR terminus of Midhurst Common being visible beyond the goods yard.

Leaving a frothy trail of smoke and steam as it emerges thankfully from the narrow bore of Midhurst tunnel, 'Vulcan' 0–6–0 no. 32527 plods eastward with the mid-week freight on 12 August 1959. In spite of damp rails and a fair load of assorted wagons, the Horsham crew brought their double-domed C2x through the tunnel without slipping.

Petworth to Midhurst in 1866 – has disappeared from view. But listen, if you will . . . listen to the wind in the trees, for even though the last train has gone there is something about this place that will be forever railway.

Satisfied with my safari into deepest Sussex, the faithful Lambretta was pointed westward on the A272, back through Rogate and Petersfield, Langrish and Bramdean, on towards Winchester. But it was not to the City station that I was bound, for this was an opportunity to travel over a

RAIL ROVER

former Great Western route and, accordingly, departure was from Chesil. Although I had missed the 12.25, there was another at 14.28 (Mondays to Fridays). With time in hand, there was a chance to look around and absorb the atmosphere of this long, narrow GWR station – so very different from the ex-LSWR emporium on the other side of the city. A steady drizzle came on, discouraging any further exploration, but I whiled away the time eating sandwiches and completing my notebook. The train started from Eastleigh, and proved to be typical of the Didcot, Newbury & Southampton line services, having an assortment of GWR corridor carriages with Collett Goods no. 2214 in charge. Though there had been no official word of forthcoming closure, recent rationalisation of train services plus a general air of surviving on borrowed time made one wonder how much

Having left the tunnel behind, Class C2x 0–6–0 no. 32534 echoes beneath the arch of the Ambersham road bridge as it returns to Pulborough through Cowdray Park on 16 June 1961 with the Midhurst goods. On this occasion though, it was running chimney-first from the branch terminus.

WEDNESDAY

In the shadow of the dense woodland of Cowdray Park, 'Vulcan' 0–6–0 no. 32522 wheezes asthmatically away from Midhurst with the branch goods on 11 June 1958. Horsham duty no. 712 was a regular working for this engine for many years; it had been the hapless victim when a culvert collapsed between Cocking and Midhurst on 19 November 1951, but was eventually recovered and repaired as good as new.

Driver's view of Petworth goods yard from the footplate of Class E4 0–6–2T no. 32470 on 4 July 1960. There was a steady trade in coal traffic here, but the station was situated two miles from the town. Today the timber building has been restored as a private dwelling.

In its final days, King's Worthy station was reduced to a single platform and ramshackle timber structure. This view was recorded on the last day of passenger services (5 March 1960), looking north.

WEDNESDAY

With Collett 2251 Class 0–6–0 no. 2214 in charge, the 14.12 from Eastleigh to Newbury steams into Winchester (Chesil) in damp conditions on 12 August 1959. The whole place bore the stamp of Swindon's regime, in total contrast to the main Southern station at Winchester City.

longer things could continue; in fact, it was to be the only season in which Rail Rover travel was possible, for passenger traffic ceased after 5 March 1960.

The three-coach train was booked to stop at all stations: King's Worthy, Worthy Down Halt, Sutton Scotney, Whitchurch Town, Litchfield, Burghclere, Highclere, Woodhay and then Newbury, the 26¼ miles taking one hour and eight minutes. It was interesting, once the train had cleared the tunnel at the northern end of Chesil station, to sample Swindon engineering for a change. Though the Southern Region had a fair number of 0–6–0 tender locomotives still active, few if any were rostered regularly for passenger duties, whereas on the Western Region the taper-boiler 2251

Though most passenger trains were in the hands of Collett Goods 0–6–0s, 'Mogul' 2–6–0s were by no means uncommon. No. 6302 was in charge of the 14.12 from Eastleigh on the final day, its staccato exhaust audible for a considerable distance as it headed north for Newbury.

Green-liveried Standard 4MT 4–6–0 no. 75024 blasts out of Burghclere on 12 September 1959 with the 12.07 Eastleigh–Newbury train. This type of locomotive was probably the most modern to be employed on passenger traffic over the DN & S line.

Tanker trains meet at Burghclere: Class U 2–6–0 no. 31794 waits in the Down platform with the 10.00 empties from Denham while a brace of 'Moguls' (4MT no. 76011 and another 'U', 31795) bring a loaded train up from Bevois Park towards Didcot on 5 March 1960. For some years after closure to passengers, the DN & S line handled regular oil-tank traffic, with even 9F 2–10–0 locomotives being noted as far south as Eastleigh.

In the deep cutting beneath the A34 trunk road between Highclere and Burghclere, Collett Goods no. 3210 gets into its stride with the 12.25 Newbury–Eastleigh service on 12 September 1959. Firemen needed to take care at this point to avoid lineside fires – hence the signs showing a black tree on a yellow circle on either side of the single track.

Though not included in the Rail Rover ticket, Lambourn branch trains (such as there were!) could be seen in their own bay at Newbury. On 27 June 1959 Pannier tank no. 9763 ambles away from the minute station at Speen with the 11.15 Lambourn–Newbury service, comprised of a single corridor coach. Note the minor level crossing and period oil lamps.

Sixty-year old 'Greyhound' Class T9 4–4–0 no. 30729 was rostered for the afternoon Oxford–Eastleigh train on 12 August 1959. Photographed in far from ideal conditions at Newbury's Down Main platform, the veteran Drummond engine gave a lively performance with a typical DN & S line train of three former Great Western corridor carriages.

Thundering through Newbury in purposeful fashion, diesel-hydraulic D800 *Sir Brian Robertson* heads the 15.30 Paddington–Penzance express on 12 August 1959. This locomotive was the first of the 'Warship' class to be built at Swindon the previous year. The head-code discs are reminiscent of Southern steam practice.

Class worked such trains daily. With driving wheels of only 5ft. 2in. diameter, 2214 was a busy little engine that gave an impression of travelling somewhat faster than reality, but in the prevailing weather perhaps that was no bad thing. With a load of just 100 tons, it had no difficulty keeping to the schedule despite some long uphill stretches at 1 in 106 both before Sutton Scotney and again after Whitchurch. As might have been anticipated, arrival at Newbury was 'right time'.

Because of the rain, there was no incentive to wander into the town and get wet while waiting for a train back to Winchester. Likewise, it was not practicable to include a round trip on the Lambourn branch (not covered by the Rail Rover ticket) as connections were not well arranged; a pity, for in the event passenger services were discontinued from 4 January 1960, so I never did manage to ride on the line. On the few occasions when I had seen the Lambourn train, it consisted of a 57xx 0–6–0PT and one or two carriages. In the circumstances, it seemed best to stay put on the platform

WEDNESDAY

until the 16.32 departure and hope there might be a few passing trains on the Berks & Hants main line. Having been gratifyingly absent for the Midhurst visit in the morning, Murphy's Law decreed there should be but one express to see – and nothing else! It is, perhaps, a measure of my desperation to record something on film that afternoon that I took the photograph regardless of it being a diesel at the sharp end of the 15.30 Paddington–Penzance. Such locomotives were still sufficiently rare to warrant a curious glance, at least, and I was rewarded with the very first of the Swindon-built diesel-hydraulics, D800 *Sir Brian Robertson*, himself. Not long after, the 15.38 from Didcot (which originated at Oxford) rolled

Struggling northward single-handed, 4MT 2–6–0 no. 76027 surrenders the tablet from Whitchurch Town on arrival at Burghclere before taking the 14.59 Bevois Park to Spondon train of loaded tankers on towards Newbury. In the Down platform T9 'Greyhound' no. 30729 makes ready for a quick getaway with the delayed Oxford–Eastleigh service on 12 August 1959.

Raring to go, Drummond T9 no. 30729 has built up a good head of steam while waiting for the road at Burghclere with the Oxford–Eastleigh service on 12 August 1959. The damp conditions and lack of a pilot loco have delayed the loaded oil tank train from Bevois Park (Southampton).

into the platform loop, being allowed fourteen minutes grace before departure south.

After the comparative disappointment of the diesel-hydraulic, the reader can imagine my amazement and delight when the Oxford–Eastleigh service was powered by none other than a 60-year-old ex-LSWR 'Greyhound' 4–4–0. First task was to try to get a reasonable picture, by no means easy in the 'available darkness' beneath the Down platform's canopy. It was accomplished from the Up platform, where the lack of sunshine on this occasion actually worked in a photographer's favour. Then it was back over the footbridge, spoiled for choice of compartments in the front coach; as ever, an older GWR example with sepia pictures and comfortable cushions. One awaited the moment of departure with pleasant anticipation, it being a local engine based either at Fratton or at Eastleigh for as long as I could remember. However, the existence of a six-wheel tender indicated no. 30729 had spent some part

Emerging into the daylight at Winchester (Chesil) on 27 February 1960, the 09.08 Newbury–Eastleigh passenger train is powered by one of the ubiquitous little Collett Goods 0–6–0s, no. 2240. The same engine was in use a week later for the final public services over the DN & S line.

Amid a good selection of GWR lower-quadrant signals, Churchward-designed 'Mogul' no. 6313 accelerates the 12.25 Newbury–Eastleigh service away from Winchester (Chesil) on 27 February 1960. All normal passenger traffic was suspended one week later.

of its earlier career on Kent Coast duties, for those transferred to the Eastern Section on loan had been required to relinquish their eight-wheel 'Watercart' tenders, probably during the 1930s. The reason was, quite simply, that the eight-wheel tenders made the locomotives too long to be accommodated on erstwhile 'Chatham' turntables. A Drummond 4-4-0 was capable of producing a unique series of sounds that set it apart from other machines, and as steam was directed into the two inside cylinders the engine would appear to stagger away, for all the world like a drunken man – but not so. To commence oscillation of 6ft. 7in. driving wheels needed a lot of effort, but once they had begun to roll then acceleration with a modest load could be quite sprightly. It would be easy to wax eloquent on the pleasures of a journey with an old T9, but I'll try to be brief and give a factual account of that homecoming to Winchester Chesil all those years ago.

With hoarse exhaust and piercing whistle, no one could have been in doubt that the all-stations Oxford to Eastleigh service was leaving. The combination of three GWR carriages and a Southern engine is not as incongruous as it sounds, for 'Greyhounds' had been drafted on to cross-country trains with great success since the twenties; as late as 1957 one or two might be found on Portsmouth to Bristol semi-fast services, loaded up to six coaches in the then fashionable 'Blood and Custard' colours. All went well with 30729 until Burghclere. There the lower-quadrant starter beside the wartime brick signal cabin remained at danger. A quick check with the timetable revealed nothing due in the opposite direction, so it could only be a freight on the 6¼-mile single line section from Whitchurch Town: the intermediate box at Litchfield had been taken out of use some time ago. The delay was a pity, but such things are an inherent problem on single lines with passing places. As the rain eased to a barely perceptible precipitation, I stepped off to speak to the crew and was able to obtain a photograph while we all waited. A feather of steam could be discerned in the distance and, in a while, it was possible to make out the high running-plate and tapered boiler of a BR Standard design. Tablets were exchanged with commendable slickness, and 76027 was opened up to some purpose to increase the momentum of its fully laden (but unfitted) oil tankers; the day of air-braked 100-tonne monster tankers was still some distance away! What none of us knew then was that the oil trains would have a virtual monopoly of the Didcot, Newbury & South-ampton route in a few short months, when the passenger services were axed.

Faced with an impossible task so far as making up time was concerned, the crew could have been forgiven for making no particular effort thereafter, but not a bit of it! 30729 had accumulated a good head of steam in the interim so, the moment the semaphore dropped, the 'Greyhound' was off. The fireman leaned well out to pick up the tablet and then the sparks began to fly. If a 'Right time' arrival was impracticable, it was through no fault of engine or crew. Scuttling along with an almost continuous roar, it was wise to beware of smuts and cinders raining down on any passenger who had the temerity to poke his head out of the window. The fireman had clearly been indentured in the Drummond principle of 'little and often', for boiler pressure was kept demonstrably close to the 175p.s.i. maximum. Odd minutes were clipped off the deficit here and there, for it was full ahead for 'Greyfriars' (Winchester). For almost six miles between Whitchurch and Sutton Scotney, the T9 gathered up its skirts (so to speak!) and broke into a gallop across the open downs. After the down-at-heel station of King's Worthy there was a shrill blast on the whistle that must have been heard a mile away at Chesil, before the train was swallowed up in the inky blackness. As it reappeared in daylight, another engine hissed impatiently in the Up platform with the 16.53 from Southampton Terminus to Newbury – it had been delayed just three minutes. Time for a momentary wave from the grinning crew, the regulator was yanked open and the aged 'Greyhound' gave tongue, its familiar voice echoing round the cutting as it headed home.

LOWLANDS AND ISLANDS

When contemplating a week's holiday on the Southern Region, I had some clear objectives in my mind whilst seeking to keep things as flexible as possible, to allow for weather conditions, traffic flows, etc. Since the very idea of a holiday in the south was inconceivable without visiting the Isle of Wight, one day had been set aside – but not a Saturday! The prospect of two-way queues of families crossing the Solent was just too much, so it was left to any other *fine* day. Thursday, 13 August 1959 dawned bright – where better to go than Ryde? The Rail Rover ticket included the Southern's steamship operations across the Solent, both from Portsmouth and from Lymington, but while frequent trains met the ferry at Ryde there was no railway connection left at Yarmouth; the Freshwater, Yarmouth & Newport branch had ceased on 21 September 1953. Thus the die was cast for a ferry crossing from Portsmouth Harbour and, in summertime, the earlier the better.

Although there were only three ways out of Fareham by passenger train, so that inevitably one covered some of the same ground several times during the course of the week, it was probable that variety of motive power would compensate for any repetition of route. So it proved that Thursday morning: the 09.10 from Southampton Central, which had produced D1 no. 31735 on Monday, offered the prospect of another 4–4–0 to Portsmouth. This time it was a Drummond T9 engine, just like the example used between Newbury and Winchester Chesil the previous evening save for being fitted with the original 'Watercart' tender. No. 30120 was another of the 1899-built locomotives to be based at

Eastleigh, and rather a favourite of mine. For those with time to stand and stare, it was the second Drummond machine to pass through Fareham before 10 o'clock that morning, for a Class 700 'Black Motor' 0–6–0 no. 30690 had trundled by with the daily Gosport goods. The thirty-strong class had been built by Dubs of Glasgow in 1897, two years before the first T9, yet it was not until 1963 that the last examples were finally withdrawn.

Fareham station was built on the first London & South Western Railway branch line, to Gosport, in 1841. Part of the early station has survived, although the distinctive chimneys of Sir William Tite's design seen in this picture no longer exist. On 22 July 1961, almost 120 years after the line was opened, Drummond '700' 0–6–0 no. 30316 eases the Gosport goods out of Fareham's Platform 4; the engine itself was 64 years old, having been much renumbered even in LSWR days (716; 459; 316).

THURSDAY

In the meantime, 30120 set about its non-stop run to Fratton with singular zest. The train consisted of five ex-LMS corridors, borrowed from somewhere, particularly comfortable after a staple diet of Eastleigh-built DMUs and a very civilised way to start the day. When the climb from Delme Viaduct had been surmounted and speed rose through Portchester, the veteran seemed to be going like clockwork. Coasting through Cosham, the extra-long connecting rods emitted their special resonance, which echoed back from the platform buildings to advise anyone who cared to listen that a Drummond engine was still active in the area. As I was going to catch the ferry, it was not necessary to change at Fratton; after much slamming of doors, the green flag gave a final opportunity to open up

The route to the Isle of Wight favoured by Queen Victoria was via Gosport; a private station was built for her, within the RN Clarence Yard. This 1980s view of Sir William Tite's terminus, a listed building, although derelict, captures something of its classic features. When trains ventured into Clarence Yard the level crossing gates were swung across Spring Garden Lane (and Mumby Road) to ensure safe passage.

before reaching the end of the journey. The engine had come to rest in the normal spot, just beneath the footbridge, where generations of steam locomotives had stopped over the years, and any slight inaccuracy with opening the regulator could result in frantic wheelspin on the greasy rails. The crew knew what they were about, however, for after letting steam into the cylinders the regulator was almost closed again until slight momentum took 30120 clear of the tricky patch; then it was opened up to some purpose and the old 'Greyhound' staggered away in familiar fashion. Beneath Fratton Bridge, beside Sydenham Terrace, under Somers Road Bridge and below Canal Walk four running lines were in parallel,

Coasting down to Fareham with steam to spare, 'Greyhound' no. 30120 passes the outer Home signal with an assorted bunch of ex-LMS corridor carriages forming the 09.10 Southampton Central–Portsmouth & Southsea service on 14 August 1959 – elderly 4–4–0s enjoyed something of a swansong that summer! From the headcode discs, this working appears to have been part of Eastleigh's 287 duty. Who would have imagined the same engine still operating between Alresford and Alton in the 1980s?

THURSDAY

before the High Level tracks veered away up the ramp and the others divided into five platform faces plus some empty stock sidings; the T9 nosed cautiously into Platform 4, wheels squealing and couplings grunting, the coda of a steam symphony whose origins were firmly rooted in the nineteenth century.

As platform space was at a premium, with other trains scheduled thick and fast, I ventured to wait at the end of Platform 5 to record any empty stock movements, being quite surprised when the 'dolly' (ground signal, mounted just below the starting semaphore bracket) was pulled off. After a warning whistle, 30120 began to reverse its own stock out of the Low Level, back towards Fratton – talk about DIY! There was a need to get my skates on if I was not to miss the 10.35 sailing to Ryde, and I had to reach

On 29 June 1960, Class T9 4–4–0 no. 30707 whisks the 10.57 Salisbury–Portsmouth vans through Hilsea Halt, passing 2-BIL unit 2027 on a stopping service to Waterloo. By this time 30707 was the last active 'Greyhound' in the Hampshire area, the other examples having been sent to the West Country to help out in Devon and on the North Cornwall lines.

With the ground signal indicating 'Clear', T9 'Greyhound' no. 30120 evacuates Platform 4 at Portsmouth & Southsea (Low Level) with the empty stock of the 09.10 from Southampton Central on 13 August 1959. There was formerly a siding between platforms 4 and 5, the only two to remain at the Low Level station today.

In between all the passenger and ECS workings, an occasional goods train had to run the gauntlet from Fratton Yard to HM Dockyard. The route necessitated running 'wrong line' up the steep ramp to Portsmouth & Southsea (High Level), through Platform 6 and then on to the sharply curving (and steeply graded) branch to Unicorn Gate. On 22 October 1959 the old 'Brighton' E1 Class 0–6–0T no. 32694 was entrusted with the task and is seen leaving Fratton beneath the ornate covered footbridge used by generations of Pompey football supporters.

THURSDAY

the Harbour Station first. Transferring to the High Level, Platform 7, any train would take me to the Harbour terminal three quarters of a mile along the embankment. Most through trains from Waterloo were scheduled to make connections with the Isle of Wight ships, and this was no exception. There was quite a crowd this fine morning as the electric unloaded at the Harbour station, nearly all heading for the Island. By comparison with the families, I was travelling light and soon got aboard one of the three diesel vessels built at Dumbarton in the late 1940s; the pre-war ships were all coal-fired paddlers.

With a great hoot the vessel cast off and left its berth to make a slow turn across the harbour, with its ever-changing naval scene – Watering Island, Clarence Yard, HMS *Dolphin* – before sailing out through the narrow

A nostalgic scene from the old Somers Road bridge: the four-coach portion from Portsmouth & Southsea–Plymouth (Friary) has just left the Low Level station at 12.15 and is echoing in the cutting below Canal Walk with 'Greyhound' 4–4–0 no. 30120 in command, passing a set of 4-COR electric units bound for Portsmouth Harbour on 30 September 1959.

From the deck of MV *Brading*, passengers had a grandstand view of PS *Ryde* churning the water before berthing at Portsmouth Harbour on 13 August 1959. During the summer season, certain sailings used to call at Clarence and South Parade Piers on route to Ryde Pier Head; these more leisurely journeys were ideal for the older paddle steamers such as *Sandown*, *Ryde* or the massive *Whippingham*.

entrance past Old Portsmouth and Southsea Castle. Thirty minutes were allowed then, a sea voyage at leisure past Spit Sand Fort before veering round to the west to berth at the end of Ryde Pier. As the mooring ropes were being made fast, a pleasant voice over the loudspeakers bid everyone welcome and gave details of the waiting trains. Services ran from the Pier Head to Brading, Sandown, Shanklin, Wroxall and Ventnor in the south or to Ashey, Haven Street, Newport, Mill Hill and Cowes on the north coast; all trains stopped at Ryde Esplanade and St John's Road stations. In addition, a tramway ran parallel to the railway tracks for those who wished to avoid the walk along the pier. But the star attraction for many

Two pairs of four-wheeled tramcars plied up and down Ryde Pier in addition to the normal train services. Though originally petrol, they were converted to diesel as an economy measure after World War II. Painted green, they were operated by the railway company on parallel tracks from the Esplanade to the Pier Head until electrification of the Island's remaining railway system rendered them redundant in 1967.

Ryde Pier Head boasted four platform faces and, in summer, the signalman was kept busy handling up to five trains per hour in and out. Class O2 0–4–4T no. 33 *Bembridge* has the road to depart from the terminus with a train for Newport and Cowes.

people, not just enthusiasts, was the Edwardian steam railway (the engines themselves were positively Victorian). Practically every one was a relic of William Adams' design for a small tank engine for the LSWR dating from 1889, transferred to the island in batches after formation of the Southern Railway in 1923, the last two being sent over in 1949 after Nationalisation. Modified with larger bunker and Westinghouse air braking, the O2 Class had proved to be the ideal locomotive for short but intensive working required by the island branches. By 1959 only the Cowes and Ventnor lines remained, but whilst the whole system was in effect a working museum the number of passengers carried at the height of summer was vast. Apart from their old-fashioned looks and panting pumps, each engine bore a neat brass nameplate of somewhere in the

The end of the platform at Ryde St John's Road station provided a good view of the Works alongside. While no. 32 *Bonchurch* is busy shunting, no. 25 *Godshill* slips out of the station with a Newport and Cowes service on 25 July 1961.

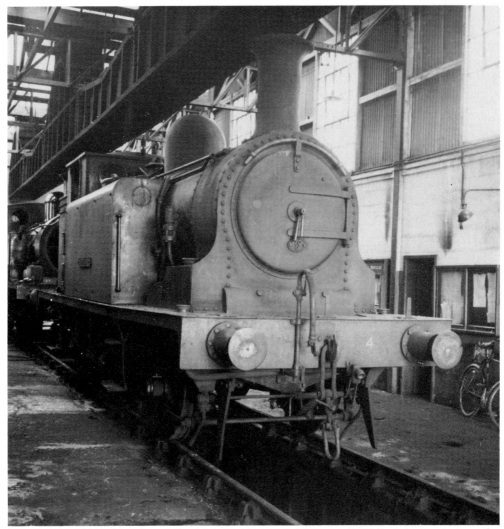

Inside Ryde shed (70H) on 13 August 1959: Class E1 0–6–0T no. 4 *Wroxall* was not in steam, being nominally based at Newport (70G). This was to be the last survivor of the Stroudley design on the Island.

Though the BR power classification of the O2 0–4–4T might not have seemed very promising – OP – this was belied by the prodigious loads they were sometimes called upon to handle on the Isle of Wight. Having virtually emptied the yard at Ryde St John's Road, no. 33 *Bembridge* gets to grips with its long train of antique goods wagons in June 1963, slowly heading up the hill towards Smallbrook Junction and the Newport line. The assortment includes no less than three brake vans. Ryde MPD is immediately behind the locomotive, partly obscured from view by the signal box.

No. 32 *Bonchurch* leaves Ryde St John's Road on another occasion in bright sunshine, shuffling off up the gradient with a more modest load of loose-coupled wagons destined for Medina Wharf on 25 July 1961.

81

No. 33 *Bembridge* takes a breather at Haven Street station while waiting for an Up train to pass in the loop. Out of season, the platform looks strangely deserted, accentuated by the fact that it is an 'island' with the station building (on the far left) separated from it by the Up track. The O2 locomotive seems to have plenty of steam available to heat the delightful, panelled non-corridor carriages on 27 March 1964.

Bird's-eye view of an 'O2' 0–4–4T taking water at Newport on 17 February 1966 – the line to Cowes closed at the end of that week. By this time the Isle of Wight railway had become unique: a living, working museum of Victorian engines and Edwardian carriages.

THURSDAY

island, a feature which over the years helped to endear them to resident and visitor alike. Of course, the lined-black livery deemed most appropriate by management on the mainland was not as attractive as Bulleid's Malachite Green (which lasted until 1952), but then Ryde Works had enough miracles to perform keeping twenty superannuated pre-1900 locomotives going without having to argue the merits of BR's livery policy as well.

Boarding a train for Ryde St John's, one had an opportunity to appreciate just how well the non-corridor rolling stock had been main-

A study in light and shade, soot and steam. No. 24 *Calbourne* has arrived at Cowes with a train from Ryde Pier Head on 26 September 1965 and is about to run round the four-coach set. This could be achieved by fly-shunting the carriages, which would then be held by the guard's hand-brake while the engine took refuge in a siding; the stock could then be allowed back into the terminus by judicious use of the hand-brake. *Calbourne* survives today in active retirement at Haven Street, together with a representative selection of the fine old carriages and some goods wagons.

RAIL ROVER

Bonchurch drifts into Ashey under light steam with a Cowes–Ryde Pier Head service during the afternoon of 13 August 1959. The overgrown siding bears silent witness to days gone by, when horse-boxes and extra passenger traffic brought prosperity to Ashey in connection with the races. Note the traditional lamp and station name-board.

tained. Seats were comfortable and well-upholstered, varnished timber gleamed and paintwork shone. Most had been modified in some way over the years to adapt to special local needs, particularly during the summer peak, but no journey was longer than 14 miles and even 40–50 year-old carriages were more comfortable than buses on switchback island roads. The Ventnor train, packed to the gunwales, was ready to leave behind no. 33 *Bembridge* and, with all the fussiness to be expected of a Victorian machine with driving wheels only 4ft. 10in. diameter, it hissed and panted its way along the pier to Esplanade station. A few hardy souls sought to clamber into an already crowded train before the guard's whistle

A classic example of an 'O2' at full stretch, as no. 31 *Chale* darkens the sky when leaving Sandown with a Ryde–Ventnor peak season train on 6 July 1960. The lattice bracket signal was provided in the days when Sandown was the junction for Newport via Merstone, but the loop was severed after closure in 1956 and the branch signal removed.

A close-up of no. 28 *Ashey* at Ryde Esplanade, with a Ventnor to Pier Head service on 27 March 1964. The specially extended bunker and cast numberplate (W28) are distinguishing features of the Isle of Wight 'O2s', while the station lamps and ornate fencing are worthy of note.

No. 20 *Shanklin* brings a Cowes train along the Pier at Ryde one summer evening in July 1963 while one of the trams sets out from Esplanade station for the same destination on a parallel track. This tranquil scene must have seemed timeless to generations of Island visitors, but how soon it all came to an end.

When the long reign of steam-power came to an end on the Isle of Wight on 31 December 1966 and conversion to third-rail electric traction was put in hand, the 'new' trains had a history of their own. On 25 August 1982, units of superannuated ex-London tube stock painted in current British Rail blue and grey livery with yellow ends and black window surrounds formed a train bound for Shanklin at Ryde Pier Head. Although two of the four platform faces have been abandoned, the station canopies have had their character enhanced by cleaner trains.

set the whole process in motion once again. This time the train was hardly on the move before it plunged into the tunnel beneath part of Ryde, to reappear in a more industrial environment near St John's Road station. Tripping over feet and assorted luggage, I stumbled out onto the platform to have a look at the hub of the island's railway network. First, I made for the Works: this was situated on the Down side of the line and offered a good position from which to photograph the following train for Newport and Cowes, powered by no. 29 *Alverstone*. Then followed the Newport goods – like everything else on the railway, its stock was antique – with no. 20 *Shanklin* in charge. I had anticipated one of the two surviving Class E1 0–6–0Ts at the head, since the quartet sent across the Solent long ago was primarily for goods traffic, but subsequent search revealed no. 4 *Wroxall* cold inside the shed. It transpired later that no. 3 *Ryde* had been

Last remaining paddle steamer of the Southern Railway, PS *Ryde* at Ryde Pier Head in 1968. Though a red funnel and British Rail blue livery above the waterline gave *Ryde* a very different appearance in its final years, none of the essential character – or appeal – was lost. Oh, for a nice leisurely cruise across the Solent on board a vessel like this. . . .

scrapped, like nos. 1 and 2 in previous years, so that ultimately the O2 Class became responsible for all traffic, including freight.

As I had travelled to Ventnor several times before and as it appeared to be the most popular line in the Kingdom this day, a trip on the Cowes route was recommended. No. 32 *Bonchurch* did the honours, taking the right fork at Smallbrook Junction and then swinging away westward in a wide arc towards Newport. On leaving the Junction the line became single immediately, with Haven Street being the only passing place in between, for Ashey had just a single platform while stations at Wootton and Whippingham had been closed in the 'purge' of September 1953. Just a rusty siding at Ashey remained as evidence of past prosperity resulting from horse-racing nearby. Newport, too, had contracted with the passage of time: not only had the rambling branch to Yarmouth and Freshwater been abandoned but, as recently as February 1956, the useful link to Sandown via Merstone had been lost. The 'branch-of-a-branch' between Merstone and Ventnor (West) was the first to go, from 15 September 1952.

Newport had also lost its Works, though the small shed (70G) continued for the time being. Beyond lay the freight sidings at Medina Wharf, Mill Hill station and the terminus at Cowes (which was in West Cowes), 93¼ miles from Waterloo.

I will not attempt to give a blow-by-blow account of the full run back from Cowes as I chose to break the journey at Ashey. Water was usually taken at Newport. One can only be thankful that something of the very special attraction of the island railways has been saved at Haven Street, and has every promise of developing in a most exciting way in future years. It is, perhaps, most appropriate that the sole survivor of Adams' gallant little O2 0–4–4T locomotives should be preserved in active condition on the Isle of Wight, where it spent more than forty years of its long official working life. So, too, have been saved several fine examples of the kind of rolling stock that was all but extinct on the mainland by the end of 1959, and even some of the amazingly quaint goods wagons. One can only regret that the potential of the Island's railways as a tourist attraction, as near in their entirety as possible, was not appreciated and acted upon before it was too late. Because of the loading gauge and weight restrictions, it was difficult to find suitable modern steam locomotives to use, although a worthy attempt to modify a Standard 2MT 2–6–2T as a replacement for the time-worn O2s in the early 1960s was aborted before it could even be tested. Instead, since 1967, only an 8-mile stump between Ryde Pier Head and Shanklin worked by erstwhile London tube trains is all that remains as a constituent of the national railway network, while even Sealink Ferries are no longer part of British Rail. All this was in the future, of course, while I rode gently back to the Pier behind a 70-year-old steam engine, with at least a chance of sailing across to Portsmouth on one of the wonderful paddle steamers, to round off the day. What price a cruise on PS *Ryde* now?

SUNSHINE OVER
THE SOMERSET & DORSET

While acknowledging the Rail Rover ticket was extremely generous, there were a few places where a slight extension of its boundaries could have simplified the planning of circular tours. For example, the former Great Western route from Weymouth was cut short at Sparkford instead of continuing to Westbury, where it could have met up with the Salisbury to Bristol line (which petered out at Dilton Marsh Halt, of all places!). One could not complain that the Somerset & Dorset line was included northwards only so far as Templecombe, since this was logical both in terms of the Southern's operating influence and also so far as making connections with the West of England main line could be effected, but it was frustrating all the same. All the spectacular northern section, with piloting from Evercreech Junction, was out of reach and some of the best trains – such as 'The Pines Express' – did not stop at Templecombe anyway. Reluctantly, therefore, it seemed best to travel over the permitted part of the route on an ordinary weekday rather than attempt it on a busy summer Saturday, so Friday, 14 August was pencilled in with that in mind.

If departure from Fareham was to be at a 'civilised' hour rather than at the crack of dawn (and the reason for this caution may become apparent during Saturday), one of the most interesting trains was by the 09.33 Portsmouth & Southsea–Cardiff General. Sometimes loaded to nine bogies, it omitted the customary Fratton stop and was scheduled to leave

Faded relic of an unforgettable railway. The Somerset & Dorset Joint Railway may have ceased to exist on 7 March 1966, but it has become known through the media of television and video to a whole new generation who never had the chance to travel between Bournemouth West and Bath (Green Park) or from Evercreech Junction to Highbridge. This particular sign stood beside a footpath across the single line between Broadstone Junction and Corfe Mullen – the 'cut-off' route – constructed in 1885 to avoid reversal of S & D trains at Wimborne.

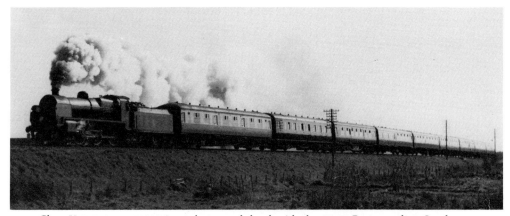

Class U 2–6–0 no. 31639 is made to work hard with the 09.33 Portsmouth & Southsea–Cardiff General service, climbing out of Cosham past the allotments on Maundy Thursday, 26 March 1959, with a load of 300 tons tare weight.

Allocated to Brighton (75A) for many years when in original condition, Bulleid 'West Country' 4–6–2 no. 34048 *Crediton* was often used on the various through services to the West. On 15 March 1958 it was noted passing Fareham East signal box whilst working the 09.40 Brighton–Bournemouth train. Having observed the permanent speed restrictions for non-stop services, *Crediton* was being opened up again as it headed west towards Southampton in familiar style.

The 10.29 stopping train from Southampton Terminus to Bournemouth Central was whisked away from Southampton Central station by Standard 4MT 2–6–0 no. 76017 on 20 February 1957. The famous gantry of semaphore signals at the western end of platforms 3, 4 and 5 managed to outlast steam by more than a decade.

Fareham at 09.53. The usual motive power was a 'Mogul', though a Bulleid Light Pacific was not unknown. Some interesting variations might occur if Salisbury turntable was out of action for repair, since the normal engine change could not then take place. In such rare circumstances, workings by both Southern and Western Region 2–6–0s between Portsmouth and Cardiff throughout could occur – 140 miles being a pretty good distance for a mixed-traffic locomotive on one tenderful of coal, although water could be taken *en route*. On this occasion the locomotive was one of the Riddles Standard 4MTs, no. 76015, which struggled a bit to maintain the very tight time of thirty minutes to Southampton Central, inclusive of intermediate stops at Netley, Woolston and St. Denys. With driving wheels of only 5ft. 3in. diameter, it excelled at acceleration from each station stop but, with 300 tons behind the tender, could not generate sufficient speed to quite keep time; the older U Class had 6ft. 0in. driving wheels, the largest of any British 'Moguls', which helped once they had 'got going'. Whilst I could have stayed on the train as far as Salisbury, a more interesting alternative was to wait at Southampton for the 09.40 Brighton–Bournemouth West service since it might produce a 'West Country' 4–6–2 or perhaps a 'Schools' 4–4–0. It was not possible to catch this train from Fareham, since it was booked non-stop from Chichester right through to Southampton. In days gone by it had produced some fascinating engines, especially four-coupled examples from classes D and L (4–4–0), I3 (4–4–2T) and H2 'Atlantic'. There had also been a run of Class 4MT 2–6–4T locomotives, both Fairburn (LMS) and BR Standard

Not all Lymington trains were push-pull sets worked by the proverbial M7. On summer Saturdays there were through services to and from London (Waterloo) that involved a change of engine at Brockenhurst. Motive power along the branch was an 0–6–0 tender locomotive, while the engine from London had to be small enough to be turned on the Brockenhurst turntable. On 23 July 1960 the 11.43 Boat Train from Lymington to Waterloo was brought into the Up loop platform at Brockenhurst by Class Q1 0–6–0 no. 33020; it handed over to 'Schools' 4–4–0 no. 30912 *Downside* for the remainder of the journey.

Although it was not unusual for some push-pull trains with limited luggage accommodation to operate with a van coupled between locomotive and carriages, it was less common to see the engine sandwiched between the van and its motor-set. On 4 June 1960 Class M7 0–4–4T no. 30060 was obliged to propel set 31 out of Wimborne with a van tacked on behind when working between Bournemouth and Brockenhurst via the 'Old Road'.

Only five push-pull sets were created from ex-LSWR 'Ironclad' corridor carriages (nos. 381–385) in 1949. Some sets were painted crimson in early BR days, but all were later finished in the standard green. Unlike the later conversions using Maunsell stock, there was no mistaking the driving trailer for a DMU. Set 385 comprised a six-compartment brake-composite (S6564S) and a seven-compartment driving trailer-brake (S3213S), seen leaving Broadstone Junction whilst working between Bournemouth and Brockenhurst via 'Castleman's Corkscrew' on 26 July 1961.

designs built at Brighton Works, that made occasional appearances on this cross-country semi-fast turn during the fifties; a long haul for a tank engine, not far short of 100 miles each way. But for the 1959 season, my money was on a Class V 4–4–0, most likely with the large diameter chimney and multiple-jet blastpipe.

Whatever the attractions of a three-cylinder 4–4–0, if one changed at Brockenhurst it would be possible to travel by the original 1847 route of the Southampton & Dorchester Railway ('Castleman's Corkscrew') and still connect with the 13.10 from Bournemouth West, providing one got out at Poole or Broadstone Junction. Much would depend on timekeeping,

Parkstone Bay, Hamworthy and Poole can be seen in this view on 2 August 1958. On this summer Saturday, a Urie H15 Class 4–6–0 (30489) has been pressed into service on the 10.10 Weymouth–Waterloo service, banked in the rear by a Drummond 0–6–0 (Class '700' no. 30695). Compared with the new record time of 2 hours between London and Weymouth achieved by electric traction on 14 April 1988, thirty years ago the 10.10 from Weymouth took 5 hours 32 minutes!

for if the push-pull service via the 'Old Road' was late the whole plan could be disrupted. The two island platforms at Brockenhurst handled very considerable traffic, but the two outer loops were mostly reserved for Lymington or Ringwood line services. There was no particular hurry here, however, for there was a clear half-hour before the next departure via the 'Old Road', due to arrive at Bournemouth West fifty-seven minutes after the Brighton train. Crossing over the long footbridge to Platform 1 (the outer face on the Up side island), an elderly M7 0–4–4T could be seen taking water, while in a few minutes a similar sight would be possible at Platform 4 when the Lymington branch train came in.

The Somerset & Dorset line had its own small sub-shed at Branksome, in the middle of the triangle of lines bounded by Bournemouth West, Branksome station and Gasworks Junction (nearest to Bournemouth Central). Typical motive power of the early British Railways period was on shed on 6 August 1955, represented by Fowler 2P 4–4–0 no. 40569 and an unidentified Stanier 5MT 4–6–0 behind. The Stanier engines were largely displaced by Standard 73xxx series locomotives from 1956 onwards, but it was always interesting to see ex-LMS designs on the South Coast.

RAIL ROVER

The biggest difficulty at Brockenhurst was the congestion that occurred on summer Saturdays over the one mile stretch of main line westward as far as Lymington Junction, since both Lymington branch and Ringwood trains somehow had to be squeezed into the bottleneck in either direction. Most services over the 'Old Road' were provided by push-pull trains composed of M7 tank and two-coach auto-set, which might vary in age from pre-World War I LSWR stock to 1922 'Ironclads' with internal corridors, interspersed with typical SECR non-corridor sets of about the same period. All but the 'Ironclads', which bore some resemblance to early Maunsell carriages but with different bogies, looked antique. Five push-pull sets numbered 381–385 had been assembled in 1949 from Brake/3rd and Brake/Composite ex-LSWR corridor stock, but these were

'Armstrong' 4F 0–6–0 no. 44558 drifts downhill from Broadstone Junction towards Creekmoor Halt with the 17.10 Templecombe–Bournemouth West local train on 4 June 1960. The usual combination of ex-LMS engine and Southern carriages has been honoured here, but Bulleid 'shortie' set 965 has displaced one of the Maunsell three-car rakes.

From 'Ironclad' push-pull unit 385 the author had an unrivalled view of Class Q 0–6–0 no. 30543 ascending Broadstone bank from Hamworthy Junction on 26 July 1961. The push-pull train was headed by Class M7 0–4–4T no. 30110 working a Bournemouth West–Brockenhurst service, while the 'Q' had charge of the 10.10 semi-fitted freight from Dorchester South to Millbrook via Wimborne.

restricted to Western Section lines such as the Seaton, Yeovil, Swanage, Bordon and Lymington branches, plus the double-track 'Old Road'. They, at least, had adequate luggage space; the older sets frequently required a van to be attached to the carriages, to the extent that some were 'piped' for push-pull gear and became almost a permanent feature of their operation during the 1950s. Some modernisation of the push-pull sets came during 1960 when older Maunsell corridor stock was adapted for motor-train working in sets of two or even three carriages. The driving trailers bore more than a passing resemblance to Hampshire diesel multiple units, and were able to replace many (but not all) of the vintage sets to be seen in these pages during the final years of steam push-pull operation.

The station announcer's recital terminated my ruminations over rolling stock and brought me back sharply to Platform 1 for the 12.08: 'Calling at Holmsley, Ringwood, Ashley Heath Halt, West Moors, Wimborne, Broadstone, Creekmoor Halt, Poole, ...' the voice being momentarily

'Change at Broadstone for the Somerset & Dorset Line.' This evocative record of the long footbridge at Broadstone Junction station shows the splendid sign pointing to the central island platform. The sign for the far (western) platform is blank, as only one passenger train normally ran between Hamworthy Junction and Broadstone. (J. Courtney Haydon.)

FRIDAY

interrupted by a rush of steam as the locomotive was prepared for its 30-mile gallop. At the appointed time the Drummond tank cleared its tubes with a great 'whoosh' and set off, snaking across the tracks to take up its proper position on the Down main line. Priming a bit, it plodded up the 1 in 176/200 gradient amid the New Forest trees, to pass Lymington Junction signal box before forking right into more open country where both roads and people were few. As far as Holmsley the tracks remained more or less straight, with Wilverley Inclosure screening the train from the main Christchurch road until it had dived beneath it.

Today, Holmsley has been largely restored from the dereliction into which it lapsed after closure on 4 May 1964 to find a new role as a

Trains in all directions. While the 10.10 Dorchester South–Millbrook goods sets off for Wimborne behind 'Q' 30543, a push-pull service from Brockenhurst sidles in with 'M7' 30031 leading. Note the long-wheelbase van sandwiched between the tank engine and its motor-train, and one of the pairs of fine 'gallows' signals to be found at Broadstone Junction.

tearoom; a road now follows the course of the railway at this point, with the building and a few trees standing like an oasis amid a concrete jungle. Beyond, the railway twisted and turned in very open country until it reached the important market town of Ringwood. Some years before, I had travelled there by the school train from Brockenhurst, when the compartment had been full to overflowing with homeward-bound pupils from the well-known grammar school, whom we used to play at cricket. Apart from a bay platform with miniature trainshed, there was little sign of the branch to Christchurch via Hurn, which closed in September 1935, although Ringwood station itself was an imposing building on the Up side.

After crossing the River Avon on a low girder bridge, the route became much more wooded. In Southern days a concrete halt was built at Ashley Heath, adjoining the level crossing, midway between Ringwood and West Moors. Military sidings at the last-mentioned station justified retention of the track after closure for a few more years. It was here, too, that the cross-country line from Salisbury came in from the north, with stations at Downton, Breamore, Fordingbridge, Daggons Road and Verwood; all but Daggons Road were built for the opening on 20 December 1866. For part of its 23 miles from Salisbury it followed the Avon valley, but then swung south-westward over heathland past the spot where three counties (Wiltshire, Hampshire and Dorset) meet, to the junction with the 'Old Road'. There followed a further 4½ miles meandering before the tracks curved decisively south into the important town of Wimborne, famous for its beautiful minster and one-time junction for the Somerset & Dorset line. For, strange though it may seem today, Wimborne was the starting point for the Dorset Central Railway, which opened the first stage of its proposed route as far as Blandford on 1 November 1860. The snag was the junction faced the wrong direction! While it remained a mere branch of 10 miles or so, perhaps it was of no account, but once the link with the Somerset Central Railway had been forged and through trains could run from Burnham-on-Sea to Poole (i.e. Hamworthy Quay station), then the delays caused by reversal at Wimborne began to loom large. A cut-off line was built to avoid the problem in 1885 and, after 11 July 1920, no more passenger trains from the S & D came to Wimborne at all. One or two bridge abutments and an overgrown embankment near Corfe Mullen are all that remain of the 1860 formation, but nothing of this could be seen from the push-pull train as it dived beneath the Poole road in a cutting and made for Broadstone.

Looking at my watch, I calculated it would be safe enough to continue

With headlamps correctly set for an S & D passenger train, 2MT 2–6–2T no. 41248 swings across the junction at Broadstone at the head of a Bournemouth West–Templecombe service on 18 April 1960. No cab-side tablet-catching apparatus was fitted to this engine, so the fireman had to lean out and take the single-line token by hand. The attractive yellow brick shelter on the island platform and distinctive footbridge can be seen on the right of the picture.

to Poole before changing on to the 13.10 Bournemouth West–Bristol train; it would also provide an opportunity to climb the unremitting 1 in 75 of Broadstone Bank with the S & D outfit, some compensation for being unable to sample the switchback over the Mendips. I left the train at Poole's curving platform, hurrying to cross over the lattice footbridge in time for the Bristol service on the other side – one could not be sure which was the 'Up' and which the 'Down' side, since a good case could then be made for either! What was beyond doubt was that the level crossing gates were opening again .... Local trains between Bournemouth West and Bath (Green Park), some of which continued to Bristol (Temple Meads), needed to be the preserve of tender locomotives in order to have adequate supplies of coal and water for what was a very exacting 72-mile journey, whereas the less demanding southern part as far as Templecombe could

With the 'gallows' junction signal obscured from view by the box, the lineside observer on 4 June 1960 was rewarded by the sight of an 'Armstrong' 4F 0–6–0 rostered for the 11.50 Bournemouth West–Bristol (Temple Meads) service. No. 44561 snakes across the points with its curious entourage before tackling the 1 in 97 gradient across the golf course between Broadstone and Corfe Mullen.

comfortably be worked by Ivatt 2MT 2–6–2Ts. There were still sufficient numbers of 2P 4–4–0 locomotives based on the S & D for them to appear at Branksome shed on local duties during 1959, although their priority task on summer Saturdays was as pilot engines for the many holiday trains over the Mendips. In the event, though, the 13.10 to Bristol was in the care of a 4F 'Armstrong' 0–6–0, five of which had been constructed specially for the line in 1922. Their S & D numbers, 57–61, became 4557, etc. on being taken into LMS stock in 1930, while British Railways merely added a further 4 at the front.

The train included a typical Maunsell three-coach set – the combination of S & D/LMS locomotive coupled to Southern rolling stock was a time-honoured arrangement peculiar to the line – that guaranteed a comfortable ride. The use of 0–6–0 tender engines for passenger traffic on a cross-country route like this was similar to operations on the Didcot, Newbury & Southampton line, although their employment on summer

FRIDAY

Saturdays on through holiday services (either as train engine or as pilot) was far from commonplace anywhere but on the S & D. All the Armstrongs were right-hand drive engines, as were at least a couple of the LMS-built 4Fs at work on the line, but there were some left-hand drive examples also (e.g. 44417, 44422/4) which rarely seemed to stray south of Templecombe. Normal whistles were fitted to both 2P and 4F locos, but there was a certain indefinable difference about the exhaust note from anything Southern, a detail that was accentuated when tackling the restart from Creekmoor Halt at the foot of Broadstone bank. With driving wheels as large as 5ft. 3in., the Armstrongs were as well equipped for passenger use as the Riddles 4MT 2–6–0s, although one was more conscious of a fore-and-aft 'surge' with the 0–6–0. Whatever reputation they may have had for being tricky to fire, from the passenger's viewpoint an S & D 4F seemed to have no difficulty coping with an all-stations duty such as this.

With Broadstone bank surmounted, the tablet catcher was set while passengers got off and on at the station. Of the four platforms at Broadstone, only two were in regular use for services to and from Bournemouth; the other two platforms were utilized very little, certainly not on a daily basis except for a few weeks in high summer, for trains to Weymouth or Swanage that avoided Bournemouth. One could see the purpose of a right-hand drive engine when leaving Broadstone, since the 'gallows' junction signal was positioned in front of the signal box, not on the island platform. There were two matching pairs of 'gallows' junction signals, both retaining LSWR-style lower quadrant arms, at the northern end of the station – very uncommon. Now the ageing Armstrong was ready, and it sidled out gently to pick up the tablet for the single line across the golf course to Corfe Mullen Junction, the 1885 cut-off to bypass Wimborne. It plodded up the 1 in 97, then coasted downhill merrily enough before surrendering the tablet at the end of the first single-line section. Over the level crossing with the Dorchester road, taken at the skew, it was then easy going to Bailey Gate. The next 6¼ miles to Blandford could be reeled off without interruption, for the two intermediate halts at Spetisbury and Charlton Marshall had been closed (with Corfe Mullen) at the end of the 1956 summer season.

Blandford (or Blandford Forum, to give its proper title) marked the end of the double track section until Templecombe; it had also been the original terminus of the Dorset Central Railway and was the most imposing station on the line. The exhaust sounded muffled as the engine tackled the stiff 1 in 80 up through the cutting, but was soon swinging away once it was over the top. Another closed halt (Stourpaine &

RAIL ROVER

Durweston) was passed in the meadows, then the gradient began to tell against the locomotive as it toiled mostly uphill towards Templecombe. There was Shillingstone, where the railway crossed the River Stour on a girder bridge; then came Sturminster Newton, with a string of cattle vans over in the yard, and Stalbridge. It was at Stalbridge that the 08.55 Bournemouth West–Templecombe (Monday to Friday) stopping passenger train was shunted, after arrival, into the adjoining Down platform to enable the 'Pines Express' to overtake. Finally, there was Henstridge, a small station alongside the single line which somehow managed to justify not only remaining open but also staffed, until the end.

Still climbing, the 4F eased beneath the West of England main line before puffing gently through Templecombe (Lower) platform, past the small motive power depot and its line of spare engines, until it was clear of No.2 Junction. Another engine was attached at the rear to pilot the train backwards into Templecombe (Upper) station, alongside the Salisbury–Exeter racetrack, where it was not uncommon for Bulleid Pacifics to hurtle through non-stop in either direction, howling like banshees. As I stepped out on to the island platform, the announcer was already intoning the form: '. . . cross over the footbridge to Platform 1 for the Exeter and Plymouth service, calling at Sherborne, Yeovil Junction, Axminster, Exeter Central, Exeter St David's, Okehampton, Tavistock, Bere Alston, Devonport and Plymouth. Change at Yeovil Junction for Yeovil Town, change at Exeter Central for Exmouth, Barnstaple Junction and Ilfracombe. Platform 2 for the stopping train to Salisbury and connections to Waterloo.' I waited to see the Brighton–Plymouth train leave at 14.39 then, almost at once, the S & D local to Bath and Bristol slipped out of Platform 3; apart from sounds of distant shunting in the Upper Yard, Templecombe was then quiet.

As there was a clear half-hour or so before the stopping train to Salisbury, I guessed there might be time for a quick look at the engine shed. It was a tidy step along the road, so I should only have a few minutes there and need to keep a watchful eye on the clock. Approaching from the road, one noticed first the mellow building that was once the Dorset Central Railway station, latterly serving as the shedmaster's office. Beyond was a 50ft. diameter turntable, with the modern two-road engine shed behind. Further on still lay the former Lower Yard with its complex of sidings, and No.2 Junction Signal Box. At this time of year there were only a couple of engines in steam on shed, with another pair stored out of use alongside the single track from the south. Here at last was a 2P 4–4–0, but this was hardly a typical S & D example. No. 40537 was a survivor from the older Midland Railway breed, being a Fowler rebuild with driving wheels of a massive 7ft. 0½in. diameter, not quite what one would expect for gradients as steep as 1 in 50. The Somerset & Dorset had had such engines before, as 40505 and 40509 had been active on local passenger services in the first years after Nationalisation, while in its independent days there had been five 7ft. 0½in. 4–4–0s on the books. Whatever the historical precedents, 40537 did not see much use after its transfer to 71H and ended its days with a full tender of coal, stored beneath the road bridge over the former spur to the LSWR main line, the last of its kind in the south; it was scrapped in 1962 and none survive today.

Time to go back to the station. The 13.10 from Exeter Central was booked to stop at all stations to Salisbury, just the sort of job for an old 4–4–0, but in the event it was a mixed-traffic Maunsell 4–6–0 of Class S15. These engines normally worked all the heaviest freights, but some

With class 'A' headlamps in position instead of the more usual S & D passenger code, 'West Country' 4–6–2 no. 34105 *Swanage* sweeps past the closed Charlton Marshall Halt with a summer Saturday express for Bournemouth West on 8 August 1959.

A late-afternoon local train from Templecombe to Bournemouth West puffs purposefully over the level crossing at Stalbridge, and is about to collect the single-line tablet from the special Whitaker apparatus on the far right of the picture. 4F 0–6–0 no. 44561 is coupled to three-coach Maunsell set no. 395, a well-established S & D combination, on 28 March 1959.

balancing duties involved relatively light passenger trains (the prerogative of 'King Arthur' locos before their withdrawal). With so much power available, the carriage couplings and springs grunted and groaned in harmony with the deep exhaust note of the Maunsell engine, while the initial surges caused the compartment door to click shut! In no time I must have dropped off to sleep under the subtle influence of such 'music', for I saw nothing of Gillingham, Semley, Tisbury, Dinton or Wilton South. 'All change please, all change!' Even before my brain was in gear, I had opened the door and tumbled out to find myself at Salisbury. There was not sufficient time to attempt a visit to the shed on this occasion, for it was situated nearly half a mile away, just beyond the point where the former Great Western route to Bath and Bristol diverged from the Southern's West of England main line. There was no Wilton Junction then: Wilton North might have been closed from 19 September 1955, but Wilton South remained open for business even if it basked in the reflected glory of the vanished 'Devon Belle' Pullman (which used to stop there in the Down direction to change engines). 72B was an interesting depot, for it played

FRIDAY

host to locomotives from both Southern and Western Regions as well as having an allocation of its own. Visitors could include Churchward-designed 2–8–0s from South Wales, as well as the expected 4–6–0s for passenger traffic. One rare arrival that day was a Hawksworth 0–6–0PT locomotive on freight; the few tank engines that reached Salisbury via the Westbury route were generally 2–8–0T or 2–8–2T designs deputising for the more usual 28xx, not humble Panniers.

The 17.08 from Salisbury was provided by one of the Hampshire diesel multiple unit fleet, which called at every station and halt (bar Redbridge and Millbrook). But, after the impressive rides behind steam, it was no anti-climax to end the day with a diesel. End the day, did I say? In essence, yes, but Saturday was to begin . . . Well, let me just say that after a good meal and a couple of hours' relaxation, it was time to return to Fareham station for a real marathon!

NIGHT TRAIN
TO NORTH CORNWALL

Waiting on Platform 3, lit only by the hoarse glare of gas lamps, time itself seemed to have stood still. Not even the arrival of the 23.27 Portsmouth & Southsea–Southampton Central diesel set could dispel that image for, with much slamming of doors, its passengers disembarked and the unit growled away towards Swanwick. An upper-quadrant semaphore clattered back to the horizontal, its oil lamp glowing red in the darkness; midnight approached. But the day was not quite done, for by my side some mailbags betokened more activity yet. A remote bell began to ring incessantly in the distance, then was heard the gentle hiss of steam, punctuated by the staccato rhythm of six-foot driving wheels on the diamond crossing just south of the station, announcing the arrival of the 23.32 from Portsmouth & Southsea to Eastleigh. The dim outline of a U Class 'Mogul' shot past me, brake-blocks squealing their lament as the last train of the day paused at Fareham. Snatching up my impedimenta, I bundled into a softly-lit Bulleid composite and settled comfortably in a corner. Muffled coughs from the sharp end matched by alternate grunts and sighs from the suspension indicated the journey had begun while, in the world outside, the bell was now silent.

The 'U-Boat' 2–6–0 shuffled along at a steady pace; all around every-thing was black and still. A dim glow inside Knowle Junction box signalled someone else was awake, but Botley was no more than a blur in the night. Then it was brake-blocks time again before the train ground to a

The original Dorset Central Railway station at Templecombe fulfilled in later years the role of shedmaster's office. In this picture on 22 July 1961 the last 2P 4–4–0 with 7ft. 0½in. driving wheels on the S & D was stored behind the building, together with a Collett Goods 0–6–0 imported by the Western Region. No. 40537 remained in store at Templecombe after all the other 2P 4–4–0s on the line had been taken away for scrap, but it never steamed again.

With some comfortable ex-LMS carriages in tow, Standard 5MT 4–6–0 no. 73049 takes the left-hand track at Templecombe No. 2 Junction and heads south with a relief to the 'Pines Express' on 28 March 1959. The double track to the left of the picture provides the link to Templecombe (Upper) and the Southern main line station.

The 16.15 Templecombe–Bath (Green Park) local train gets a clear signal and heads northward behind an exuberant 2P 4–4–0, no. 40563, on 28 March 1959. This was the first of Fowler's 6ft. 9in. two-cylinder 4–4–0s to be built at Derby in 1928.

Free-steaming as ever, rebuilt 'West Country' 4–6–2 no. 34096 *Trevone* eases forward gently at Templecombe with the 11.30 Brighton–Plymouth through train (including four carriages from Portsmouth) on 26 July 1961. The Brighton engine would have been replaced at Salisbury, so *Trevone* is fresh and raring to go with only three stops before Exeter Central (59½ miles). Note the old cattle van.

Although its paintwork looks a bit shabby, Class S15 4–6–0 no. 30841 could be relied upon to keep time. Having shunted its train clear of the main line to enable another to overtake, the Maunsell locomotive draws its Bulleid three-coach set (788) back into the Up platform at Templecombe before continuing to Salisbury with the 13.18 Exeter Central–Salisbury local service on 22 July 1961.

dead stand outside the silent Locomotive Works at Eastleigh. Minutes passed as it waited for the road; idly, I wondered which engine it was. Silently, the signal changed from red to green and, all at once, the train began to move forward. In rather asthmatical fashion the engine crossed the complex junction and drew into Platform 1. 'All change!', bellowed an unseen porter with sudden enthusiasm; reluctantly, I stirred myself and got out. The timetable had been silent on the subject of cross-country connections at such an hour, and the best I could divine so early on a Saturday morning was the 01.50 to Yeovil Town. With one and a half hours at my disposal, periodic perambulations round the brooding station alternating with short spells in the smoke-filled waiting room for warmth

If one was able to obtain permission to visit Salisbury shed (72B), it could provide some very interesting sights. On the turntable behind the main shed building the massive bulk of 2–8–2T no. 7202 was slowly rotating on 4 October 1958 – a visitor from the South Wales valleys, having arrived on a lengthy coal train earlier in the day.

SATURDAY

kept me awake until shortly before 2 o'clock. Where the devil was that train? Doing my best to insulate myself against the stale fumes of the waiting room, even the periodic snores of its incumbents had a soporific effect at last – the sandman was calling.

To my jaded senses the sandman seemed to be making too much noise! Jerking into wakefulness, it became apparent that someone was trying to wake all the sleeping beauties in the waiting room. In a panic, I looked at my watch: it was five minutes past two, so could this be the Yeovil service? Like a large kettle on the boil, no. 31790 steamed into Platform 2 – was this the Yeovil train? The guard confirmed my anxious question, whereupon I was able to find the same compartment I had been occupying earlier (pity I couldn't have stayed there all the time). But now the

On 14 August 1959 Hawksworth taper-boiler 0–6–0PT no. 8479 brought a freight into Salisbury from the Westbury line – a very rare appearance of this type of engine in the area. No. 8479 was shedded at Bristol (St Philips Marsh) at the time, no more than fifty miles away.

Catching the last rays of the evening sunlight, 'Battle of Britain' 4–6–2 no. 34055 *Fighter Pilot* spins its wheels in true Bulleid style with the 18.35 Bournemouth West–Brighton as it curves away eastward at Fareham on 11 July 1961. The author was privileged to take this dramatic picture from the steps of Fareham West signal box, an excellent vantage point long since vanished. Westbound trains approaching Fareham from Cosham triggered a warning bell mounted on the original Tite station building, which only ceased ringing as the locomotive reached the diamond crossing alongside *Fighter Pilot*.

Before the double-track route avoiding Funtley tunnel was plagued by a landslip (which led, ultimately, to its abandonment), 'Lord Nelson' 4–6–0 no. 30851 *Sir Francis Drake* tops the summit of the 1 in 100 gradient from Fareham with the 11.08 Fratton–Eastleigh empty stock train on 4 October 1961. Until displaced from top-link duties in their final years, this type of locomotive was seldom to be found in the Portsmouth area, but the ECS duty could be arduous and required a powerful 4–6–0 to surmount the adverse gradients out of Cosham and Fareham.

situation had changed: gone was the lethargy of its preamble from Portsmouth, for 31790 was positively sizzling with the incentive of starting nearly twenty minutes behind schedule. The 01.50 was booked non-stop to Salisbury, and all thoughts of sleep were banished as the rebuilt 'River' class engine (once a 2–6–4T belonging to the SECR) fairly rattled along, leaving a trail of frothy, white steam in the still night air. Chandler's Ford, Romsey, Dunbridge and Dean were like ghosts in the darkness, then past Milford goods to the sharp curve at Tunnel Junction, through the murk beyond until Salisbury was in sight – what a scintillating run it had been, to be sure!

Though I would like to have stayed aboard as far as Yeovil Junction, it

Only rarely was Eastleigh Works opened to the public, although some private parties were admitted. Inside the erecting shop on 3 March 1956 was a brace of 'King Arthur' 4–6–0 locomotives undergoing repair: no. 30770 *Sir Prianius* and 30805 *Sir Constantine* were still employed on top-link tasks at this period, the latter coupled to a six-wheeled tender. The livery was Brunswick Green lined out in orange and black.

was by no means certain I could have made the intended connection there as neither of the following through services were scheduled to stop anywhere between Salisbury and Exeter. As I stood near the end of the long Down platform with my camera, timetable and provisions, the magic of a steam train at night was imprinted for ever in my memory as the old 'Mogul' hissed away up the hill and out of sight; at its present gait it would be home in Yeovil by four. Meantime, there was more excitement for the 01.10 from Waterloo would soon be due. On normal weekdays that service conveyed through carriages for a whole gamut of destinations in the west, but during the summer peak a separate train ran at 01.20 on Saturdays with through carriages for Plymouth and Padstow only. In

Some indication of the severity of the curve past Salisbury Tunnel Junction signal box can be gained from this elevated view, showing double-chimney 4MT 4–6–0 no. 75070 in charge of an excursion on 20 March 1966. The main Waterloo–Salisbury and West of England line ran behind the box while, in the 1980s, the single track Laverstock curve has been reinstated to form a triangle.

Rebuilt 'Merchant Navy' 4–6–2 no. 35004 *Cunard White Star* lifts a heavy West of England express from London (Waterloo) past Salisbury MPD during daylight hours on 4 October 1958; it was this engine that powered the 01.20 newspaper and mail train for Plymouth and Padstow on 15 August 1959, in which the author rode as far as Wadebridge.

Howling like a banshee, 'Merchant Navy' Pacific no. 35025 *Brocklebank Line* tears through Crewkerne with the 07.30 Exeter Central–Waterloo service on 30 July 1960. Some years before, at this very spot, another 'Merchant Navy' loco (35020 *Bibby Line*) had come to grief when a driving axle suffered metal fatigue. The outcome was the rebuilding of the entire class of 'Merchant Navy' 4–6–2s, plus half of the Light Pacific engines with 'West Country' or 'Battle of Britain' names, without oil bath and air-smoothed casing; Walschaert's valve gear was fitted in place of Bulleid's own patent type.

RAIL ROVER

deference to the sleeping populace of the City of Salisbury, no hoot was emitted as the first of the two night trains from Waterloo approached, but the unique sounds of valve gear, connecting rods and exhaust advertised the presence of a Bulleid Pacific just as faithfully as any crow on the whistle. One of the rebuilt 'West Country' class was in charge, through coaches being conveyed to Ilfracombe and Bideford only, dividing at Barnstaple Junction. After taking water, the ghostly 4–6–2 eased forward, slipping briefly, then with increasing confidence it began to accelerate, emitting syncopated sounds that only a musician could have composed before disappearing into the distance.

Another long-lived LSWR species was the Adams 'Radial' 4–4–2T, two of which monopolised the Lyme Regis branch until 1946, when a third example was re-acquired to help out. One of those engines that had soldiered on for many years was 3520, renumbered 30584 by British Railways in 1948 and finally retired in 1960. Still wearing its 'rampant lion' insignia on the side tanks on 3 August 1959, 30584 was running round at Axminster before tackling the 1 in 40 gradient again towards Lyme Regis. Axminster's Up platform and bay are no longer in use and the footbridge has gone; the branch closed from 29 November 1965.

SATURDAY

Close on its heels appeared the 01.20 from Waterloo with rebuilt 'Merchant Navy' 35004 *Cunard White Star* at the head. This service was well patronised, although not over full, and the compartments felt warm. Water was taken, for the Southern had no troughs like the other regions of British Railways, and then the big engine took charge. After the inevitable slight slip on the wet and greasy rails by the water crane, *Cunard White Star* crept forward deceptively; a light touch on the regulator produced another momentary slither before the free-steaming Bulleid boiler was shrieking with excess power. Slowly, unerringly, the massive machine began to talk, being well into its stride by the time it echoed past the engine shed and turntable at the foot of the climb up towards Wilton.

To convey something of the 'mystique' of a major railway station by night (and because my equipment didn't run to achieving an adequate result in steam days), this is Exeter St David's in the diesel age. 'Crompton' diesel-electric locomotive 33.001 has been rostered for a night train to Waterloo on 25 November 1978 while the puddles glisten in the harsh glare of modern lighting; only the simmering of steam is missing.

RAIL ROVER

Inside the shed a number of dark dinosaurs could be discerned in the gloom, hissing and bubbling in anticipation of the morrow; they did not seem to be an endangered species, then . . .

With the light switch on 'Dim', the cosy compartment tempted me to sleep. Although the train was not scheduled to stop before Exeter Central, in fact it shunted off one or two vans at rural stations on the way; I was remarkably incurious as to which they were! In spite of this, 35004 managed to drift downhill past St James' Park Halt into Central Station almost exactly to time. As 'Merchant Navy' locos were not allowed to

Having double-headed the 01.10 Waterloo–West of England train between Exeter Central and Okehampton, Drummond 'T9' 4–4–0 no. 30338 (with wide cab and without coupling-rod splashers) idles its time in the yard as the sun peeps over the Devon hills and bathes the carriages in golden light. The two-coach Maunsell set and aged locomotive will form the 07.00 departure from Okehampton for Plymouth (Friary). This was to be one of the last occasions on which the author witnessed a 'Greyhound' at work in the west; the date is 8 July 1960.

Halwill Junction at 7.00 a.m.: an early train for Bude is being prepared in the bay with Standard 3MT 2–6–2T no. 82019 in command, while the remains of the 01.10 Waterloo–Padstow (one Bulleid carriage and one bogie newspaper van) brood in the main platform behind Class N 2–6–0 no. 31839 on 8 July 1960. It was much too early for the Torrington branch to be stirring.

venture much further into the wild and woolly west, I had a few moments in which to stretch my legs while the changeover took place. In the east was the pink glow of dawn, with the promise of a fine day ahead. Refreshed by a carton of 'cardboard milk' for 1s. 0d. (5p) from the machine on the platform, I climbed back into the nice warm Maunsell carriage for the next stage of the journey knowing that 'Battle of Britain' 4–6–2 no. 34063 *229 Squadron* was on the front. Snaking down the 1 in 37 gradient to St David's Station, for a moment one had a panoramic view of the slumbering city still cold and grey, for the sun's rays had not yet pierced beyond the distant hills. As usual, progress was checked on entering Western Region territory, followed by a brief pause in the station itself. Satisfied the interloper could continue, the Bulleid 'Spam Can' demurely slipped out in order to regain Southern metals after Cowley Bridge Junction. Then it was away like the wind, to arrive at Okehampton with time in hand.

The North Cornwall line on 28 July 1961, its last summer under Southern control: 8.00 a.m. at Launceston. The overnight mail and newspaper train from London, the 01.10 from Waterloo, waits in the Down platform to continue its long journey to the end of the line at Padstow while empty stock has come up from Wadebridge to form the 08.20 Launceston–Okehampton service, with 'N' 2–6–0 no. 31846 at the front.

While the newspapers are unloaded and a mail van waits for any post, Class U 2–6–0 no. 31791 indulges in a little shunting at Port Isaac Road station on 15 August 1959. A couple of horse-boxes are being collected from the small yard before being attached at the front of the 01.20 Waterloo–Padstow service, a relic of the days when British Railways handled every kind of traffic one could imagine.

SATURDAY

At 06.09 the Pacific departed with the Plymouth stock, leaving very little in the platform for onward transmission to Padstow. For a while nothing happened, which was not so remarkable as everything seemed to be more leisurely as one progressed further into the west; according to the timetable, the Padstow portion was not due to leave until 06.30. Just in the nick of time, a 'Mogul' came down from the shed and attached itself to the handful of bogies, all that was left of the 01.20 from Waterloo. I was surprised it was another U Class, no. 31791, for west of Exeter was generally reckoned to be N Class country, these being rather more flexible with slightly smaller driving wheels for the steep undulations attributed

Port Isaac Road had a deserted air when a single diesel railcar arrived on an Okehampton–Padstow duty on 19 September 1966. By this time the Western Region had taken over, the summer visitors had mostly gone and closure (between Wadebridge and Meldon Junction, Okehampton) was only a fortnight away. W55017 had been built for the Western Region in 1958 by the Gloucester Railway Carriage & Wagon Company, a type that later became Class 122.

to Devon and Cornwall. The stately pace of this operation was all allowed
for in the timetable, and eventually 31791 and its diminutive load ambled
away up the hill to Meldon Quarry, rumbling over the spindly viaduct
before settling down to a steady jog along the single line through
Maddaford Moor and Ashbury to Halwill Junction. What a remote spot it
was! Yet, even at this early hour a Standard 3MT 2–6–2T, no. 82011, was
in the yard shunting. It was due to take the local out for Bude at the same
moment as the Padstow train was scheduled to depart, 07.15, which gave
the latter time to acquire another couple of carriages from a siding.

   With a more respectable load once more, the 01.20 Waterloo–Padstow
swept sharply away to the left and then began to trundle along, stopping
at every station: Ashwater, Tower Hill, Launceston. Having ground to a

Sole exponent of the 'square splasher' variety of 2–4–0WT locomotive designed by W.G.
Beattie in 1874, no. 30586 was engaged in some light shunting at Wadebridge on 15 August
1959. With its two contemporaries (30585/7), it was very largely responsible for the author's
overnight journey to North Cornwall.

'Small Prairie' 2–6–2T no. 5557 raises the echoes on leaving Wadebridge with the 09.08 Padstow–Bodmin General and Bodmin Road on 15 August 1959. In the background the 01.20 Waterloo–Padstow train slips away on the final leg of its long journey, while '0298' Class well tank no. 30586 pauses demurely alongside the coaling stage during a lull in performing duty 634.

Few passenger duties remained for the mainland 'O2' 0–4–4Ts by the end of the fifties, but 30199 (and two-coach Maunsell set 199) were employed on the 09.48 from Wadebridge to Bodmin North on 15 August 1959. The Southern and Western Region services between Wadebridge and Bodmin shared a common route as far as Boscarne Junction.

Getting into its stride, 2–6–2T no. 5570 follows the single track to Boscarne Junction from Wadebridge with the 09.08 Padstow–Bodmin General service on 8 July 1960; then, the Southern's North Cornwall line to Launceston and Okehampton ran parallel for about a mile.

stop at the last-mentioned town, it seemed as if we were stuck there as nothing was happening. Another peep at the timetable reminded me that this was a Saturday, when the train was scheduled to wait 18 minutes in order to allow empty stock to clear the line from Wadebridge. There was just enough light to obtain a picture of the archetypal North Cornwall line train of N Class 2–6–0, two carriages and a van shuffling in before a shrill blast summoned me back to my compartment; it was 08.05, and we were due to leave. Thereafter, basking in the growing warmth of the sun streaming in through the window and lulled by the unhurried orderliness of it all, I must confess I dozed off and slept remarkably soundly. The peaceful rhythm was disturbed by much screeching of brakes and banging of doors as we stopped at Port Isaac Road. Now the air was invigorating with the salt tang of an Atlantic breeze, while the little station seemed alive with people. There was an unmistakable bump from the front, and to my astonishment 31791 detached itself and reversed across a double-slip

SATURDAY

into the tiny goods yard to retrieve a brace of horse-boxes required elsewhere. Then, reunited with the carriages, 31791 and its entourage bowled along the home stretch through St Kew Highway down to Wadebridge. Though this was not the final port of call – quite – the sight of a genuine 1870s 2–4–0WT on station pilot duty was enough to tempt me out of my comfortable compartment without a second thought.

The last time I had come across one of these antiques was during a tour

One of the most endearing memories of a visit to North Cornwall was the sight of an aged Beattie well tank on the Wenford goods. Its boiler dappled by sunshine filtering through the trees, no. 30587 bustles along through Dunmere woods with china clay empties on 8 July 1960, performing duty 637 from Wadebridge. Built in 1874 as LSWR no. 298, it was put on the duplicate list as 0298 when Drummond introduced his first 4–4–0 locomotives (C8 Class) in 1897. The Southern Railway later renumbered it 3298, while its BR number was allocated in 1948. Remaining active until December 1962, it is now preserved as part of the national collection.

of Eastleigh Works in February 1957, stripped down for a major overhaul. Now, here was the same engine, 30586, shuffling along with a couple of coal trucks for the shed yard, eighty-four years old and as spry as a bird! After more than nine hours of travel (the last six on the same train, give or take the periodic pauses), it was like the climax of a pilgrimage; never before had I been to see the aged Beatties in their native habitat. The first of W. G. Beattie's little 2–4–0 well-tanks to be exiled from London Suburbia to the wilds of North Cornwall arrived in 1893, and it is still remarkable to think that a trio of those quaint locomotives outlived their sisters by sixty years, lingering in capital stock until the final month of 1962. But in 1959 no one seriously thought of their replacement, so it seemed, for inside the shed stood the other two (nos. 30585/7) waiting for their weekday duties on the

One of the original series of 'Small Prairie' 2–6–2Ts designed by Churchward for the GWR, no. 4559 returns to Bodmin General light engine after bringing some china clay empties to Boscarne Junction exchange sidings on 8 July 1960. The Southern branch to Bodmin North (and the goods-only Wenford Bridge line) diverge behind the Ground Frame box.

SATURDAY

Wenford goods, in company with the 'spare' Adams O2 0–4–4T no. 30200. Near the coaling stage sizzled a pair of 'Mogul' 2–6–0s, while back at the station another O2 (30199) was being prepared for the 09.48 turn to Bodmin North. Even as I stood watching, absorbing the 'period' scene, the level crossing gates beyond the station opened and a rural train that was pure Great Western in its character squealed to a halt in Platform 2; this was the 09.08 from Padstow to Bodmin General and Bodmin Road. Swindon products being what they are, there was no disguising the presence of such a train at a very 'South Western' outpost. It snorted in that rather rude way some GWR engines have, before making a very

The pagoda platform shelter and diesel railbus are evidence of the Western Region takeover in North Cornwall in its final months. AC Cars' four-wheel railbus W79977, once based at Swindon for the two branches from Kemble, was seconded to Wadebridge for the former SR Bodmin North branch, which it worked from a specially constructed interchange platform at Boscarne Junction. The railbus paused hopefully at Dunmere Halt on 19 September 1966, but the service was withdrawn from 30 January 1967.

Showing signs of age, 'Greyhound' Class T9 4–4–0 no. 30718 issues steam from a number of places as it sets off from Wadebridge on 16 April 1960 with the final passenger train of the day, the 18.00 Padstow–Okehampton. The scorched smokebox door shows evidence of recent hard work by this engine, which spent many years based in the West Country, but it was nearly worn out and went for scrap in 1961.

The small sub-shed at Okehampton was home for no more than a couple of tender locomotives, but 'T9' 4–4–0 no. 30338 was preparing for action when seen from the 'Atlantic Coast Express' on 15 August 1959.

pointed departure south-eastward. After all the sound and fury of 'Small Prairie' 2–6–2T no. 5557, the discreet shuffle of the aged well-tank as it went about its appointed task was an object lesson in good manners!

Attention now focused on the O2 no. 30199, which occupied the loop Platform 3, coupled to set 199. This comprised two identical Maunsell Brake/Composites, a type very popular in the far west since they were equally at home on through services to Waterloo or on the long local journeys that were the essence of the North Cornwall line. Taking advantage of the brief lull in activity to walk up towards the signal cabin, one was able to enjoy the sweep of the Camel estuary beyond the yard and the occasional cries of the gulls; it was a glorious day. For some minutes I

A cloudy morning found 'West Country' 4–6–2 no. 34096 *Trevone* employed on the 09.35 Padstow–Waterloo 'Atlantic Coast Express' on 8 July 1960, comprising just a couple of Bulleid composite brakes. By this time services on the Bodmin North branch were being worked by an 0–6–0PT acquired from the Western Region, no. 4666, seen in the loop platform waiting for the 09.48 departure.

The important station at Okehampton was the junction for services to the North Cornwall line. Class N 2–6–0 no. 31837 gets away with a two-coach Maunsell set (no. 27) forming a local train to Plymouth (Friary) on 8 July 1960, while a Bulleid air-smoothed Pacific waits over in the yard with headcode discs for the Padstow line in position.

wandered around, exploring and looking for a good spot to record the O2 0–4–4T when it set off for Bodmin's Southern station. Whilst doing so, it became apparent that what looked like double track heading back towards St Kew Highway was actually two separate single lines: the nearer one was used by North Cornwall services, while the further track led to Grogley, Nanstallon and Dunmere Halts on the way to Bodmin, but with connections for Wenford (freight only, at Dunmere Junction) and the Western Region branch to Bodmin General (which curved away at Boscarne Junction). I felt sure it would be necessary to come back another time to examine them. Just the lightest crow on the whistle was enough to remind me that 30199 was about to leave, whereupon the little Adams engine gently hissed its way out of the station before crossing over onto the far track for the 6¾-mile run to Bodmin North.

Back at the station, some undemanding shunting was being performed by the veteran well-tank. Having tired of catapulting coal wagons into one another near the engine shed, 30586 found another pair of Maunsell corridors and parked them in Platform 1. Then, like an antique sewing machine, its well-oiled valve gear moved almost silently as it slipped away into the goods shed to procure a couple of small vans, attaching them to the rear of the carriages before retiring to the yard again. One could only marvel that not one, not even two but *three* of these relics had survived the vicissitudes of time for more than eighty years – easily the oldest examples of former London & South Western motive power still at work, and the last link with the two Beatties (father and son) who had largely shaped the destiny of that proud railway from 1850 until 1878.

An Up service from Plymouth (Friary) drifts into Okehampton station behind 'WC' 4–6–2 no. 34107 *Blandford Forum* on the morning of 31 July 1960. This important Devon town finally lost its passenger trains from 5 June 1972.

RAIL ROVER

Though much rebuilt, the trio of well-tanks had made the Wenford branch and its china clay traffic very much their own for generations, although it was not unknown for one of them to fill in with a short passenger train to either Bodmin North or Padstow when required. But now one of the 'Moguls' was coming off shed to take the two-coach train and attendant vans down to Padstow, forming the 10.15 (Saturdays only) service to the outpost of the Southern's empire; it was time to board.

I was not to know this was to be my one and only ride out to Padstow. In subsequent years I visited Wadebridge, saw the Beattie tanks again and again, but nevermore ambled along beside the Camel to the very end of the line, for in 1959 there was no reason to suppose it would ever close. Padstow on a summer Saturday could be quite busy, for at the guest houses and hotels it was 'changeover day' with all its attendant comings

The Down 'Atlantic Coast Express' prepares to leave Exeter Central behind a brace of Bulleid 'Spam Cans' on 14 August 1959. No. 34069 *Hawkinge* is coupled ahead of 34033 *Chard* with the Ilfracombe and Torrington portions, due to depart at 14.10 for North Devon.

and goings. The carriages on which I had travelled now became part of the august 'Atlantic Coast Express', immortalised among railway men and enthusiasts alike by its initials, 'ACE'. As such, it was no task for a mere mixed-traffic 'Mogul', for over by the turntable was a genuine un-rebuilt Bulleid Pacific being prepared for the run to Exeter. Out of season, it was possible for a T9 4–4–0 to be utilized on this service, although one was more often provided between Plymouth and Okehampton when the load was light. But today being a Saturday, the usual two-coach train had been strengthened to five, plus the two vans, so justifying a Bulleid machine throughout. No headboard was carried at this extremity of the system, but the presence of no. 34075 *264 Squadron* at the head of the train was an indication that the 11.00 departure was *the* most important service

After the demise of the specially adapted Stroudley 'E1/R' 0–6–2Ts from Devon in the late 1950s, a handful of powerful 0–8–0T locomotives was drafted in for banking duties between Exeter St David's and Central stations. This unique Maunsell design was represented by Class Z no. 30956 at Exeter Central on 8 July 1960.

As the evening shadows lengthen, 'Battle of Britain' 4–6–2 no. 34072 *257 Squadron* eases forward at Salisbury with the Down milk empties on 5 July 1960. Trainloads of these special six-wheel tank wagons, which were fully fitted and could travel at passenger train speeds, were dispersed to rural locations all over the west to be refilled with milk for London next day.

Padstow could boast. On the dot, the 'Battle of Britain' air-smoothed Pacific edged cautiously forward, avoiding the wheelslip so prevalent with the Bulleid design. By the time it reached the girder viaduct over Little Petherick Creek, the big engine was sailing along in majestic fashion; this was the way to travel home!

At the height of summer, the Padstow portion of the 'ACE' ran as a separate train on Saturdays. This arrangement was to cater for the large numbers of people travelling to and from their holiday destinations in the west, and meant that the Southern's most prestigious service in that area ran in no less than four parts. The Padstow train acquired its restaurant car at Okehampton plus a few more coaches at Exeter Central, finally reaching London's Waterloo at 17.24. While it was tempting to travel the full distance of 259¾ miles, the appeal of a bath, shave and bed with clean sheets was growing stronger. It was difficult to keep awake with 34075 swishing past country stations on the North Cornwall line, and even more so after Halwill Junction. At Meldon I looked out for the G6 0–6–0T engine kept at the Quarry for marshalling the ballast wagons (once numbered 30272, but then re-numbered into departmental stock as DS 3152), but was unlucky; it must have had weekends off, and was most likely tucked up inside the tiny shed. From the opposite window, as the train drifted downhill into Okehampton, I was rewarded with a glimpse of one of the diminishing band of Drummond 'Greyhound' 4–4–0s, as no. 30338 (one of the examples with wider splashers and cab) squatted outside the rather utilitarian sub-shed, preparing for the 13.20 to Launceston.

Satisfied that the Southern byways of the far west could still be relied upon to produce true Victorian locomotives from the drawing-boards of Beattie, Adams and Drummond, I allowed the shuffling three-cylinder exhaust beat of the Bulleid machine to lull me to sleep again.

HAYLING HIGH SUMMER

After the many hundreds of miles spent on board the trains from Monday until Saturday, Sunday was a convenient time for doing something slightly different. Not that one was tired of railways, not at all, but a little fresh air seemed just the thing. Perhaps a day by the sea? As a Portsmuthian myself, I was familiar with the dubious delights of shingle beaches and, besides, the East Southsea branch had closed somewhat before my time. No, the only place to go for sandy beaches (if not for bikini-clad girls) was South Hayling. To try and reach them by car or bus, especially if the weather was hot, was a nightmare – traffic would queue right back along the B2149, jamming Havant solid (there was no bypass for the A27 then) – and road travellers were advised to prepare themselves for a long, hot journey. But for those in the 'know', there was a simple solution: take the train.

Having slept like the dead, Sunday morning presented an opportunity to relax nearer home before returning to the office (and preparation for more exams) next day. Holy Communion at 8 o'clock, followed by breakfast with a gentle ride over Portsdown Hill by the quieter back roads to Havant was a pleasant prelude, yet even by 10 o'clock the crowds were building up. I parked the Lambretta on the north side of the station, thankful that it took up so little space and cost next to nothing to be left there all day. Once on the platform I could see that the first train for Hayling was quite well loaded and would soon be preparing to leave (it didn't depart until 10.05 on summer Sundays). Over the footbridge, modernised like the rest of the station for electrification of the Waterloo

In their later years, some Brighton 'Terriers' were overhauled at Eastleigh Works. Freshly painted, no. 32662 was almost dwarfed by much more modern motive power outside Eastleigh shed (71A) on 31 March 1961. Note no spark arrester fitted on top of the chimney.

Leaving Havant with a typical out-of-season load of just two coaches, Class A1x 0–6–0T no. 32677 takes out the 11.35 for Hayling Island on 14 October 1958. Although one of the new high-capacity BR Standard non-corridor carriages is coupled behind the engine, the brake/composite at the rear is none other than a former LSWR corridor vehicle. By contrast, in the goods yard opposite stands an equivalent non-corridor carriage transferred to the departmental stock.

141

Also without spark arrester, the original Class A1x 0–6–0T (built as an A1 in 1872) latterly numbered 32636 stands in the roundhouse at Fratton on 23 December 1959, out of use. Next door, also out of steam, was Class G6 0–6–0T no. 30349 (formerly of Guildford). The 'Terrier' retired in November 1963 after working the final train to Hayling Island, aged ninety-one, but has since found plenty to do on the Bluebell Railway in its native Sussex.

Just for a moment on 22 July 1962, it was possible to see three 'A1x' 0–6–0Ts at Havant at the same time. Priming heavily, 32640 prepares to leave from the bay platform as soon as the connecting train of 4-COR 'Nelson' electric stock has unloaded its passengers from London, while nos. 32646 and 32650 wait for a clear road to cross over. No. 32640 has charge of the first service to Hayling on this Sunday, the 10.35, while 32650 will work the 11.05; 32646 will remain spare at Havant until 32640 returns.

With two Bulleid 'shortie' corridor coaches, Class A1x no. 32677 bustles past the double fixed Distant signals between Langston and Havant with an Up train from Hayling Island on 30 June 1959. This engine had an enlarged bunker, evidence of its years on the Isle of Wight.

and Brighton services in 1937/8, the bay platform contained an anachronism from the previous century. It wasn't that the carriages were any more ancient than some I had used the preceding day, it was the motive power that was so positively Victorian! Stroudley's diminutive 'Terriers' had appeared on Hayling services before 1900, and remained in charge almost without exception until that sad day in November 1963 when all traffic was withdrawn; even then it was the first two 'Terriers' to be built at Brighton Works ninety-one years before that headed the final train. As there were no tunnels and only one road overbridge, modernisation of the passenger stock had not remained stunted as it had on the Isle of Wight, but sharp curves and a long timber viaduct across Langstone Harbour restricted the choice of locomotives to just two types beyond that point. True, one or two sporadic attempts were made to use ex-SECR P Class 0–6–0Ts, I've been told, but it was the rebuilt Stroudley A1x tanks that soldiered on into ripe old age. The casual observer who walked down the platform to look at the funny little engine would be struck by the disparity in size between it and the carriages, for they towered above the midget so that its buffers had to be mounted higher than the frames in order to be on a par. In typical Brighton fashion, the Westinghouse pump wheezed and thumped in syncopated rhythm from time to time while the locomotive waited at the platform, reminding one of a peppery old gentleman impatient of delay.

143

The old station nameboard shows the spelling to be 'Langston', although most maps indicate the surrounding area as Langstone – just one of the curiosities of the Hayling railway! But, while road traffic queues up at the level crossing, Class A1x 0–6–0T no. 32646 and its train pause only a moment or two before continuing on their journey with an Up train for Havant on 18 May 1959. This particular locomotive is still at work, having returned to the Isle of Wight since preservation.

Class A1x 0–6–0T no. 32670 follows the shoreline at Langston with a Havant–Hayling Island train only six months before closure. The disused harbour siding, rusted and forgotten, can be discerned curving away from the branch before the train approaches the timber viaduct. This locomotive is also preserved, having returned to the Kent & East Sussex Railway where it spent many years before Nationalisation.

144

SUNDAY

The summer Sunday ritual was for a second set of carriages for the Hayling branch to be brought up from Fratton shortly before the first departed; for those well-informed it was a sight worth seeing, for it was invariably double-headed by a brace of 'Terriers'. They would wait in the Up platform loop until all was clear, before scuttling across on to the branch with almost indecent haste, to set the carriages back into the bay. One Alx would then detach itself from the entourage and wait until the other had completed its shunting movement, before running back into the loop pending its turn to take over the train. With three engines and two sets of coaches it was possible to run a half-hourly service and keep one loco at Havant to coal up between journeys. The timetable provided alternate fast and slow trains, the former running non-stop to or from Hayling and the latter calling at both Langston and North Hayling en route, taking ten and thirteen minutes respectively. This resulted in four trains per hour using the single line, for there were no intermediate passing places, which kept the crossing keeper at Langston station busy. It was at Langston (note the differing spelling of the station from the Harbour, the latter sporting a final 'e') that the rail traveller could observe the hapless motorists queueing on either side of the level crossing gates, for until that point the train had kept well away from view, just drifting down the meandering track after the very minor level crossing by the signal box at Havant, beneath the old A27 and past the watercress beds near Wade Court. As the crossing gates were being re-opened to road traffic for the next stage of the crawl to the coast, whichever 'Terrier' was in charge would give a peremptory whistle and let fly.

Whatever hollowness might be associated with the average Brighton exhaust, the echoing note produced by a long tapering chimney such as was fitted to most of the Alx Class was heard to best effect at this spot. Surrounded by trees on either hand, the exhaust echoed back and forth as the little locomotive strained its utmost to get the train moving well before the long timber viaduct necessitated circumspection. As the trees thinned, the train curved one way and then the other past the site of disused sidings as it advanced towards the foreshore. Here, broken concrete blocks kept the sea at bay, while ahead lay the impressive bridge with its opening girder span and controlling signal cabin. Opening of the span became rare after World War II, but a protective Home signal was provided just in case. The lattice post also exhibited a fixed Distant arm on the opposite side, the third such double-arm signal post to be found on the line; a double-fixed Distant stood near the watercress beds between Havant and Langston, while an identical Home and fixed Distant combin-

Mirror image of the Hayling train. On a still winter day, 'A1x' no. 32661 rumbles slowly across the old timber viaduct at low tide with the 11.55 Up service to Havant in January 1963. The roads were treacherous with snow and ice, but the little train managed to keep going to provide a link between Hayling Island and the rest of the world in Arctic conditions.

A favourite study of 32677 approaching the Hayling terminus on 18 May 1959 – everything except the coaching stock seems to be to a smaller scale! This 'Terrier' was returned to the mainland from the Isle of Wight in 1949, for a short time running in Malachite Green with 'British Railways' in 'Sunshine' style lettering on the tank sides. A decade later it still looks very smart, with copper-capped chimney, but unfortunately it did not survive into preservation.

ation occurred on leaving Langston station. Rumbling gently over the bridge was an interesting experience, especially at high tide, for it seemed as if the tiny train had gone to sea. The official limit over the structure was 20m.p.h., but once beyond the corresponding Home signal protecting the bridge from the south there was not far to go to North Hayling. The Home signals on either shore were normally left in the 'line clear' position whatever the direction of travel, since their sole function was connected with the infrequent opening of the bridge.

The unstaffed halt at North Hayling was on the very edge of the western shore, where oyster beds once flourished; at high tide the place had more in common with Exton or Lympstone on the Exmouth branch than anywhere else in Hampshire! The final couple of miles past fields and open country brought the visitor to Hayling Island terminus, which had opened for business in July 1867. Trains normally ran into the main platform, which had a run-round loop, but at weekends matters did not rest there. With a second set of carriages in use, it was necessary to shunt the stock into the bay after the running round had been accomplished, to

Skirting the western shore, close to where the oyster beds used to be, 'Terrier' no. 32650 approaches North Hayling Halt with the 14.58 mixed train from Hayling Island to Havant on 14 May 1963. This service was allowed seventeen minutes for the full journey instead of the usual thirteen, presumably to allow for any shunting at Langston. No. 32650 is another of the Stroudley design to have survived into active preservation.

Class A1x no. 32661 being coaled by hand at Hayling Island on 4 March 1960. A pair of Bulleid corridor coaches stand in the main platform while a spare occupies the bay; the yard is full of coal wagons. No. 32661 was preparing for the 14.53 'mixed' back to Havant, when the two carriages in the main platform would be coupled ahead of the wagons in the loop before the whole entourage could be despatched north to the 'mainland'.

While another 'Terrier' departs from Hayling Island terminus with a train for Havant on 15 June 1958, 'A1x' 0–6–0T no. 32640 has been running round its coaches in the main platform. No. 32640 at some stage has been equipped with a LSWR chimney, as well as other non-Brighton modifications, but at this period both platform starting signals were genuine LBSCR relics.

make room for the next arrival. In the meantime, passengers streamed off the train towards the barrier, intent on making their way to the island's chief attraction, its wonderful sandy beaches. Most would be content to walk half a mile along the tree-lined Staunton Avenue opposite the station, but in summer an open-top bus was operated periodically by Southdown between Hayling Ferry, Beachlands and Eastoke.

Childhood recollections of Hayling in high summer conjure up scenes of interminable traffic queues, two-hour journeys by bus (having waited an equal number of hours to board one!) for a distance of just 5 miles, acres of sand and sunburn. In 1949 or 1950 there is a memory of a Malachite Green A1x (one of those repatriated from the Isle of Wight, probably no. 32677) at work on the branch, but otherwise all the engines were painted black with the usual passenger lining. Among those one can recall are nos. 32636 (the original Stroudley 'Terrier'), 32640 (the Gold Medal winner, formerly *Brighton*), 32646 (which was sold in 1903 to the

End of the line. Having changed the points, 'A1x' 32670 was about to run round its train in the main platform at Hayling Island on 12 May 1963 before returning to Havant. Alongside is the disused end-loading dock while opposite, the 'Station Stores' is well placed to cater for the needs of day trippers and holidaymakers. Sadly, this was the final season for the Hayling branch and the duties of Stroudley 'Terriers' on British Railways.

The only form of public transport now on Hayling is the bus, but this open-top Guy 'Arab' ceased operating in September 1963 – just weeks before the railway closed. Southdown Motor Services took delivery of no. 466 (GUF 166) in July 1945, right at the end of the war, and rebuilt it with an open top for the 1951 season; it was a Portsmouth area vehicle throughout its life. Service 149 ran from Hayling Ferry to Eastoke during the summer only, via the railway station and Beachlands. The former 'Utility' bus is seen passing Hayling station on 5 August 1962, when crowds of passengers had just arrived by train.

LSWR and had a very varied career), 32650, 32655 (*Stepney* of Bluebell Railway fame), 32661, 32662, 32670 (re-acquired from the Kent & East Sussex Railway upon Nationalisation), 32677 and 32678. Two more that I don't remember were 32644 and 32659, as they departed during the early 1950s (the latter became part of the Departmental stock as DS 681), but another former Lancing Carriage Works shunter did appear at Fratton for a while. This was the last un-rebuilt 'Terrier' (Class A1) in working order, DS 680, but I cannot be certain it was actually used on the Hayling line; why else would it have been in Fratton shed? A quarter of a century after closure of the branch, it is comforting to reflect that nearly all the 'Terriers' mentioned above survived into preservation, and some are still at work on private railways.

SUNDAY

Something that eluded weekend visitors to the Hayling branch was any freight activity. However, quite substantial quantities were handled at times, being attached to the first Down train or returning by the 14.53 service from the terminus, both of which were designated as 'mixed'. Up mixed trains were generally diverted from the bay into the Down main platform at Havant, to facilitate shunting of the wagons across into the yard; this task was performed by the engine of the pick-up goods, probably a 'Mogul' or 0–6–0 tender locomotive. The Up 'mixed' was allowed seventeen minutes instead of the normal thirteen for the 4½ miles to Havant although, with the possible exception of Langston siding (adjoining the approach to the road bridge, on the north side), there was no intermediate shunting involved. Perhaps the combined load of carriages and wagons sometimes exceeded the four-coach trains that were operated on summer weekends, when five hundred passengers could be disgorged onto the platforms at either end of the line!

My week of Railroving was drawing to a close. After a swim and an hour or two sunbathing – during which time the beach had become distinctly crowded – it seemed a good idea to go and 'play trains' again. With the sun at the meridian, the walk along the shaded Avenue back to the station was not to be hurried. Ahead could be discerned the brick-built goods shed and a handful of wagons, while slightly to the left another swarm of day-trippers was streaming out of the station forecourt towards the sea. In the far distance an Alx 0–6–0T was leaving bunker-first from the bay platform, but there would not be long to wait for the next; its engine was already running round the train in the main platform. By the time I had crossed the road, the assorted stock was being propelled into the bay and one was spoiled for choice of seats. Because of the short journey and the need to move the maximum number of passengers quickly, BR Standard non-corridor carriages were much in evidence at such times. A ten compartment all-third could seat one hundred and twenty full-size passengers – and a few more at a pinch! With a train consisting of three of these plus a Maunsell Brake/Composite, four hundred seats were available as well as one corridor and the residue of the Guard's compartment.

The return trip to Havant was quick, just ten minutes of non-stop running behind an octogenarian locomotive. There were still the interminable traffic jams at Langston, where the tiny engine burst into a paroxysm of activity in order to surmount the adverse gradient all the way into Havant. One could appreciate why spark arrestors had been deemed desirable on this line! Without so many bodies on board the 'Terrier' had no difficulty, and swept round the sharp curve into the station with all the aplomb it could muster. Before you could say 'William Stroudley', the engine had uncoupled and run back to take water at the column by the footbridge while, at the other end of the platform, the locomotive from the previous arrival attached itself for the next expedition to Hayling. And so on and so on . . . until the 20.05 – the last train – across to the island. It was such a useful, characterful institution that one could not imagine Hayling in summer without the train. But, like so much else of our transport heritage, it was swept away in a fit of economic zealotry that took no account of its true worth. The local communities of Havant and Hayling might have something to say about it, even now.

As I rode the scooter home, that 16 August 1959, I pondered on the past seven days. Travelling by train further than ever before (in so short a timespan), the Southern Region had taken me to Hawkhurst and Halwill, Henstridge and Haven Street, Hartfield, Holmsley and Highclere in the course of a mere week. The sharp-eyed cynics among my readers may observe I was only just in time, too, for all these places (with the possible exception of Haven Street, which has risen phoenix-like to find a new niche as the Isle of Wight Steam Centre) were closed to rail passengers during the sixties. If the purpose was to 'beat the clock' of retrenchment, the flames of which were fanned into a holocaust during the Beeching era, it could be said I had succeeded – at least in part.

But how can one share the simple pleasure of those journeys, those rural railway lines, with those who never knew them? I can only hope that the pictures in these pages will speak volumes, and that if some of our most delightful branches remain beyond the reach of travellers today, they will not be completely forgotten.

EPILOGUE

The 'option' of steam haulage anywhere on the Southern Region expired after 10 July 1967, following electrification of the Bournemouth main line. Regional Rail Rover tickets went out of fashion, too, particularly when a massive chunk of the Southern – the entire system west of Salisbury, no less – was transferred to the Western Region from 31 December 1962. No longer was it possible to travel at will anywhere from Kent to Cornwall, for the truncated Southern did not serve the latter any more. Truth to tell, those lines once presided over by the powers that be at Waterloo had soon ceased to be served by anyone at all: the lovely North Cornwall line from Okehampton closed from 3 October 1966, Padstow to Wadebridge and the various Bodmin branches following after 30 January 1967, whilst between Bere Alston and Okehampton the service was withdrawn from 6 May 1968 and thence to Yeoford (Coleford Junction) after 5 June 1972. Paddington had called the tune and, within a decade, demolished almost the complete edifice of holiday routes that it had inherited west of Exeter; small wonder that cynics referred to 'the Withered Arm'.

With the end of steam on British Railways, I found a new interest in transport matters by acquiring a vintage bus. As preserved railways and steam centres developed from erstwhile stumps of branch lines or gave new life to abandoned engine sheds, one was able to travel round to these places in a charismatic vehicle more in tune with their sentiments. There was even time to get married and have children. . . . As the sixties and seventies gave way to the eighties it was possible to look back and see it all in perspective – diesel power, dereliction and electrification – in a more dispassionate way. Steam locomotives that had been banished to Barry or various museum centres around the country were being born again, to bring the lure of hot oil and sulphurous fumes to new generations,

Yeovil, here we come! The nameplate and coat of arms of the borough were carried by Bulleid 'West Country' Class Light Pacific no. 34004, seen here in its rebuilt condition without air-smoothed casing. The locomotive became well known in its early days for, during the 1948 locomotive exchanges, it ran with an LMS tender on test in Scotland.

Fareham station in the eighties. Viewed from the north as night was closing in, a temporary footbridge was in use for a time when the old one was in need of structural repair. Although all four platforms still existed, 1 was seldom used and 3 had become a dead-end for trains terminating at Fareham (usually from Eastleigh). While 2 remained as the Down platform, 4 had become the Up line since a new bridge had been constructed in 1969 at the south end of the station. In this Sunday picture, two push-pull trains between Reading and Portsmouth (one in each direction) can be seen with Class 33/1 'Crompton' diesels and 4–TC units.

EPILOGUE

while first-generation diesels were enjoying a popularity denied them in their first flush of youth. On British Railways' own tracks in selected areas, two-, three- and four-cylinder exhaust beats were reverberating out of cuttings and beneath bridges as steam celebrated a renaissance on both private charter and short season heritage tours; the 150 Celebrations at both Shildon and Rainhill had brought their own respectability. Perhaps the time was ripe to have another look at BR?

For the American and Japanese tourists there is still an All-Line Rail Rover, but this is not something for the average family man to indulge in. However, the fortuitous coincidence of a 15-year-old son (who had just completed his GCE 'O' level exams) being interested in transport, fully justified taking a week's leave: for scarcely more than twice the cost of the original Rail Rover, I could purchase one of four limited area Runabout tickets on the Southern Region and take Miles at half fare. There were, inevitably, some restrictions on their use compared with the old Rail Rover, the worst being no travel before 09.00 on weekdays (Monday to Friday), though even that might not be insuperable . . . . Only areas 'C' and 'D' included Fareham, and although the latter was valid for travel to Portsmouth, Woking, Ascot, Reading and Bournemouth, area 'C' stretched beckoningly westward as far as Yeovil. As my son and I had just begun a model railway layout based on the Bridport branch from Maiden Newton (which happens to be situated on the Yeovil–Weymouth line), an opportunity to visit the locality by train simplified our choice. Though a trifle rusty, I soon found myself ferreting through the pages of free timetable booklets 16 and 17 as ideas for day trips began to formulate. While it was not possible to emulate any of those wonderful excursions described in the preceding pages exactly, there was just one possibility. . . .

And so it was that, just after 11 p.m. on Friday, 19 July 1985, Miles and I set out to walk to Fareham station in good time to catch the last train of the day to Southampton. Silhouetted against the harsh sodium streetlamps, one could not help noticing that the noble Tite chimneys of the original 1841 part of the structure had been reduced to meaningless remnants while, once on the platform, all the distinctive semaphore signals with their lattice posts and finials had been displaced by anonymous colour-lights, worked from a remote panel box at Eastleigh. Neither Fareham East nor West signal cabins remained, while the guttering gas lamps had given way to garish fluorescents. Something that hadn't changed very much was the approach of a Hampshire diesel-electric multiple unit, though it curved into Platform 4 (the erstwhile Gosport line) since Platform 3 had become a dead end following the bridge reconstruction of 1969. The 23.25

RAIL ROVER

Portsmouth Harbour to Southampton was provided by one of the hybrid three-car units created from an original two-coach set plus a salvaged former EMU driving trailer (unpowered) that had seen service as a Tonbridge 'Tadpole', the resultant marriage being numbered 1403. We travelled in the former electric component in the middle, having a whole compartment to ourselves that was reminiscent of generations of non-corridor stock – very quaint in the eighties. Stopping at all stations (the title 'Halt' has been expunged from British Rail parlance, despite more stations becoming unstaffed), 1403 trundled along at a modest pace: up the hill to Swanwick, down rather more steeply to the crossing of the Hamble River at Bursledon, up again and round the corner to Hamble. One could dismiss the frequent and disconcerting changes of gradient or direction as a feature of a railway built to a budget in the post-Mania economy period of the Victorian Age, but there is precious little difference in profile when the train continues beyond Netley. The 1889-built link between Fareham and Netley is no more tortuous than the

Waste not, want not. Southern Region made the most of surplus former electric driving trailers, which had been recovered from the hybrid 'Tadpole' units associated with the Reading–Redhill–Tonbridge services, by using them as centre cars for the remaining 2H 'Hampshire' sets. Renumbered 1401, one of these units reflects the evening sun as it approaches Hilsea on a Portsmouth–Reading service in 1982, painted blue and grey with yellow ends. The disused siding at this point provided a connection to the former Royal Ordnance Depot, but both this and the gas-holder in the background have now vanished.

EPILOGUE

1866 branch off the first LSWR main line at Portswood, for trains leaving St Denys station heading eastward have just as much need of a compass as those departing from Fareham!

An even blacker darkness betokened the approach to the tunnel beneath Southampton, though the actual tube is illuminated by night and day since rebuilding. At twenty-five minutes past midnight it had become Saturday as the train ran into the brightly-lit station: 'All change, please'. There were two choices now: either we settled down to wait one and a half hours for the 01.55 to Bristol (Temple Meads) to take us as far as Salisbury or we could catch the Up Mail to Basingstoke and change there; the end result would be the same. Keeping our options open, we watched the nocturnal activity at an important main-line station as mailbags were sorted and stacked on the various platforms. As we waited, the stock for the Bristol service was brought in on Platform 3 behind 'Crompton'

Southampton by night. 'Crompton; 33.011 occupies Platform 3 with the stock of the 01.55 train to Salisbury and Bristol (Temple Meads) on 20 July 1985. Note the mail-bags on the trolley alongside.

157

The flyover at Battledown, where the Bournemouth and Salisbury routes divide. Class S15 4–6–0 no. 30502 brings an Up local passenger and van train from Bournemouth West over the girder structure on 18 October 1958.

The cold light of dawn at Yeovil Junction. The fine old footbridge had been cruelly truncated and many tracks removed since steam days, and it was not easy to obtain a quality picture in the few moments available, especially against the light. No. 47.597 was about to blast off with the 01.40 Waterloo–Exeter St David's, having unloaded the newspapers and handful of passengers soon after half-past four.

EPILOGUE

———

33.011. There was a great temptation to get on board and switch off for a couple of hours, but the 22.38 Weymouth to Waterloo mail train would be due soon. At ten minutes to one it swept into Platform 2 with 33.110 in charge, quite a lengthy mixture of Standard Mk. 1 carriages and GUV bogie vans. There seemed to be a good crowd on board already, for there was a cosy warmth within, but there was no rush for the train was not booked away until 01.20.

A compartment is much preferred by those who have commuted regularly to London, for open coaches are always draughty and frequently noisy. We managed to find sufficient space in a dimly-lit compartment and dozed off for a time. Speaking for myself, I was not conscious of anything much until the train left Eastleigh with a bit of a jerk! Then, the commuter's sixth sense being locked into gear, I was aware of Winchester – briefly – before speed rose markedly through North Hampshire, past the flyover at Worting Junction and into Basingstoke. At some stage the push-pull 'Crompton' had given way to an electro-diesel machine, no. 73.106 (probably at Eastleigh), and thus provided our first ride behind one of these useful inventions. But the signal remained obdurately red, delaying the mail by some minutes until an inter-regional Freightliner (with usual 'Brush 47' power) cut across its bows to head north via Reading. Once the signal changed to green, the '73' notched up and began to move forward. Suddenly a brilliant flash lit up the sky as a break in the conductor rail caused arcing under such power. We watched until its tail lamp was no more than a distant glimmer before crossing over to the Down side, to await the 01.40 Waterloo–Exeter mail and newspaper train. This was the direct descendant of the 01.20 'Night Train to North Cornwall' experienced in 1959, and only possible for us to use because this was a Saturday morning when the 9 o'clock curfew time did not apply. A bright light in the distance resolved itself into an off-centre headlamp, which presaged the imminent arrival of another '47' on the Exeter service – but what a shadow of its former self. Whereas it had not been uncommon to find the overnight train to the West of England loaded to eighteen vehicles for passengers, mail and newspapers when I used it in the 1959–1961 period, in 1985 it amounted to little more than a quarter of that length, with just one GUV.

There was no difficulty finding an empty compartment on this train; our tickets were quickly examined and we were left in peace. Lying full-length on either side of the compartment it was simple enough to let the wheels lull one to sleep again, while the big Brush locomotive throbbed away purposefully towards the west. Andover, Salisbury, Gillingham and

———

On rare occasions the Salisbury to Exeter route has been used for diversions by Western Region services. Although Wilton (South) station closed from 7 March 1966, both the station building on the Up side and the signal box were retained, the latter in connection with the single-line section westward to Gillingham. On 4 January 1981 HST diesel unit 253.010 was obliged to wait for the single-line section to clear, in full view of the signalman at Wilton.

Beneath Summer House Hill nestled the small engine shed and the former joint Southern and Great Western station of Yeovil Town. On 3 August 1959 the shuttle service between Yeovil Junction and the Town consisted of the last surviving 'Gate' motor set 373 with Class M7 0–4–4T no. 30131. In the foreground the single track connected with the third Yeovil station at Pen Mill (on the Castle Cary–Weymouth route).

Yeovil Town station forecourt was used by Royal Blue coaches as an interchange point even after closure of the railway in 1966. On a hot summer day in 1968 a typical 'camel-back' Bristol LS6G with Eastern Coachworks styling (OTT 93: no. 1294) picks up passengers for Bournemouth. The station building was dated 1860, but now it is no more.

Sherborne were noted only for the pauses between movements of a well-performed symphony that I remembered from long ago. But, like all pieces of music, it came to an end, with someone bellowing 'Yeovil Junction' outside! Sixth sense got a rude awakening, while Miles sleep-walked out onto the platform; it would soon be dawn. Once the footbridge here had been magnificent, spanning six tracks, but 'Westernisation' (or rationalisation) had trimmed things appreciably. The turntable still survived over near the goods shed, but all the semaphores had gone and the place looked a bit forlorn in the cold light of day. Light? There might just be enough to record this epic journey, if I was quick. All fingers and thumbs in my haste, the needle on the exposure meter showed a hint of life at f1.8 with speed at 1/30/second. The horn blared momentarily, the picture was taken and 47.597 opened up like a startled rabbit, the carriages chattering over the points with increasing speed until all one could hear was the receding throb of the powerful diesel: it would be in Exeter within the hour.

It was a trifle early for the minibus connection to the Western Region station at Pen Mill so, to keep warm and make best use of the time, we started to walk there. All the activity plus the sharp morning air gave us an appetite. On reaching a wooden gate leading into a big field giving a

RAIL ROVER

distant view of Yeovil, we stopped to eat some sandwiches. Down there, near the stream, marked the place where the Town station and locomotive depot used to be, while away in the distance a branch line to Taunton once meandered through Hendford, Montacute, Martock and Langport West before meeting up with the Western main line. Amazing, now, to think the Rail Rover ticket of 1959 had included that former Great Western branch line for much of its length, but that was how the regional boundaries used to be. Now there was nothing, station and shed swept away as though they had never been, yet Yeovil Town had been well placed for passenger traffic – indeed, the forecourt provided connections by Royal Blue coaches to all parts of the west, even after closure of the station on 1 March 1967. But by 1985 Royal Blue, too, had passed into history and the station site given over to a car park.

Our repast complete, we walked on over the bridge close to where the shed had been and then scrambled down to follow the track bed of the former single line to Pen Mill Station. It didn't take long – it was only half

Branch trains from Taunton often provided a local connection between Yeovil Town and Pen Mill. Green-liveried 'Small Prairie' no. 5548 sets off along the single line to Pen Mill, only half a mile away, with the 16.22 from Taunton on Bank Holiday Monday, 3 August 1959.

EPILOGUE

a mile, after all – but I was reminded vividly of a Saturday in August 1954 when a friend and I cycled from Poole to Yeovil, and spent a little while at the small Western Region engine shed at Pen Mill (in the 'vee' between the branch to the Town and the main line to Weymouth). Designated 82E, Pen Mill shed was only a tiny affair: my friend David Millett and I had been quite miffed to find only one Pannier tank in residence, although he did take the trouble to photograph 4689 for the occasion. Five years later, the same engine found its way to Fratton when its duties on the Maiden Newton to Bridport branch were taken over by diesels – small world! Miles and I climbed up the steps by the bridge to cross the road to the station, but we were rather too early and the building was still locked. The side gate was open, so we found a place in the sun and . . . waited.

On Saturdays the first trains were scheduled to leave Pen Mill at 06.55

Early morning activity at Yeovil Pen Mill on Saturday, 20 July 1985. No. 47.515 heads the 05.10 from Bristol (Temple Meads) to Weymouth as the 06.00 Weymouth–Bristol service formed by Pressed Steel DMU L424 runs into the station from the south. The erstwhile branch to Yeovil Town curved away to the right beneath the bridge, with the tiny sub-shed straight ahead beyond the junction of the two tracks.

One of the first diesel trains to operate the Bridport branch was at the branch terminus on 1 August 1959. Built as a three-car 'Cross Country' unit by Swindon Works, this type later became Class 120. It comprised Motor Second W50694, all-Second W59425 and Motor Brake Composite W50732; the centre car had miniature Buffet facilities, which must have been rather a novelty at Bridport!

'Fill her up, please!' Push-pull equipped 'Crompton' 33.115 and 4–TC set were parked on the Quay line at Weymouth on 20 July 1985 owing to reduced facilities at the station itself, which was in the process of being drastically rebuilt. At least there shouldn't be any excuse for running short of fuel, with a service station so handy – 'Did you say a couple of hundred gallons, Guv?'

EPILOGUE

in both directions. At about half-past six there were signs of life around the station, then levers began to be pulled in the signal box making point rodding rattle and signal wires vibrate, for this part of Yeovil still rejoiced in proper semaphores and a traditional cabin. The first Down train rumbled in, forming the 05.10 Bristol (Temple Meads) to Weymouth. Loco-hauled, the '47' would no doubt later provide the motive power for one of the Saturdays only inter-regional services from the coast. We strolled over to secure seats in a compartment version of the Mk. 1 stock, but there was no hurry as the 06.00 from Weymouth was not in sight yet. Although my original Rail Rover ticket would have included travel over this line, there had not been sufficient time to take advantage of it in 1959; the same held good for the Bridport branch which, though worked with typical Western locomotives and rolling stock until the new diesel multiple units appeared, was by then under Southern dominion. And, just as former Southern branches had been lopped by Paddington in the 1960s, so Waterloo axed the Bridport branch after a long struggle in 1975; it was no good dwelling upon the mistakes of the past. A hoot heralded one of the familiar Class 117 three-car units built by Pressed Steel coming in off the single line section from Maiden Newton, an economy brought in during the seventies in an effort to stem rising costs. One feature that has not been abandoned, however, is the link between Yeovil Junction and Pen Mill constructed as a wartime measure, which runs parallel for a while until the Weymouth route dives beneath the Waterloo–Exeter main line and away into the depths of Dorset. Thornford, Yetminster and Chetnole stations remain open, but only the intermediate one is staffed. Various small halts were constructed further south in the period between the two world wars in an effort to stave off competition from buses and private cars, but all were closed in 1966. Why close an unstaffed halt on a country railway, you may ask? A good question, and one I trust British Rail will address whenever there is evidence of local need, for stations *have* been re-opened – Templecombe is a classic example – and others could follow in the future.

The large Brush diesel, 47.515, made the journey seem effortless as it powered its way towards Weymouth, calling at every station. After Dorchester West, double track returns as the erstwhile Great Western route links up with the Southern line from Bournemouth, the former junction at Upwey being the only intermediate station; the Abbotsbury branch was an early casualty, being closed from 1 December 1952. But as the approach to Weymouth is made, travellers who recall the days of steam will notice the greatest difference. At the time of our visit the

Shuffling along the quayside at Weymouth, outside-cylinder Pannier tank no. 1369 brings a Channel Islands Boat Train past an intriguing assortment of private cars on 28 April 1962. The 1366 Class was always associated with the Quay Tramway, and this particular engine escaped a scrapyard fate following a final year or two in Cornwall on the Wenford Bridge branch.

station had been reduced to a group of Portakabins and three platforms, a far cry from its role as joint terminus for both South Western and Great Western Railways since 1857. So few sidings remain that the upper section of the tramway line is sometimes used for storage. But mention of the tramway line brings to mind that very special track through Weymouth streets for more than a mile, the route to the Quay and the Channel Islands far beyond. I have never been privileged to travel over it myself, with the train nosing its way amongst the traffic like a pike in a pond, but the sight of a Boat Train negotiating the wharves and narrow streets is an unforgettable experience – especially for the road vehicles in its way!

After more breakfast and a pleasant stroll along the promenade we

Bank Holidays can be wet. On 1 May 1978 33.115 squelches along the street tramway with the 09.36 Waterloo–Weymouth Quay Boat Train, passing the Sealink ferry *Sarnia* in a steady downpour. A temporary flashing light and warning bell have been clipped on above the buffer beam.

wandered back to the station. A long Inter-regional train was standing in Platform 1, while a blackboard nearby said 'BRADFORD: 10.05'. This was the image of the summer Saturday holiday train of the eighties: whereas one might have expected to find a train for such a Yorkshire destination at Bournemouth West in the 1950s and early sixties, all set to do battle with the Mendips via the S & D with a powerful steam locomotive at the head

167

Amid the welter of shipping, fishing boats and pleasure craft in Weymouth Harbour, the Up
'Channel Islands Boat Express' steals gingerly along the Quay behind 'Crompton' 33.114 on
Saturday, 26 June 1982. Behind the locomotive is an interesting building that appears to
have some Brunel ancestry.

Waterloo to Weymouth as it was after 1967: at Bournemouth (Central) the unpowered 4–TC
sets for Weymouth were detached from the powerful 4–REP Buffet set – which was always at
the London end of the train – and coupled to a Class 33/1 locomotive for the last part of the
journey to the Dorset coast. In this scene 33.101 exhibits the head-code '91' and is making
ready to leave Bournemouth with an eight-coach load.

EPILOGUE

(7F 2–8–0 in 1959, probably a 9F 2–10–0 between 1960 and 1962), the 1985 equivalent was an ubiquitous Brush '47' and the service routed via Southampton, Basingstoke and Reading. Perhaps the point was that this summer holiday train was still running; some people still preferred to leave their cars at home and enjoy a vacation by the sea. The carriages were filling up fast, but we managed to find a couple of unreserved corner seats and made ourselves comfortable. If journeys behind Class 47s were becoming commonplace, that did not make either engine or excursion uninteresting, and 47.099 had a white roof and looked quite presentable. Nor did it disappoint, once it got under way. Leaving right on time, it soon got to grips with the rising 1 in 74 to Upwey, steepening to 1 in 50/52 near the summit of Bincombe Tunnel. There were three stops (Dorchester South, Wareham and Poole) before an electrifying climb of the 1 in 60 gradient of Parkstone Bank brought us to Bournemouth.

Happy Birthday, Bournemouth Central! On 20 July 1985 the station was celebrating its centenary, with the site of the former engine shed given over to a display of vintage cars, buses (even a trolleybus) and a fairground. Alongside stood electro-diesel 73.001, first of the type to be delivered in 1962, with the special 'Channel Islands Boat Train' title above the buffer beam, waiting for the Up 15.00 service from Weymouth Quay. It was usual to change engines at Bournemouth in view of the conductor rail thence to London. No. 73.001 was so clean it might have been taking part in the 100th birthday event!

RAIL ROVER

Something special was afoot. Outside in the forecourt there were some fairground organs, a selection of vintage Bournemouth Corporation vehicles (including a trolleybus) and some beautifully restored old cars, so what was it all about? On enquiry, it transpired that the fine station building – which I always knew as Bournemouth Central – was celebrating its centenary, having been opened to traffic on 20 July 1885. While it may have lost its engine shed (71B) and had the two centre tracks removed after electrification, the place continued to exude railway atmosphere. One can only trust that it will continue to fulfil its function, and take the forthcoming extension of electrification to Weymouth in its stride.

At this point it is appropriate to step down and look back over the past

The 12.56 from Weymouth was a rather curious train, routed via Bournemouth, Southampton, Eastleigh, Romsey and Salisbury on its way to Bristol (Temple Meads), including a section of line primarily used by freight traffic through Chandler's Ford. Composed of two different types of DMU, the service operated only until the end of August. Class 117 three-car Pressed Steel unit B434 was leading two-car BRCW Class 101 unit C801 on 20 July 1985 at Salisbury.

EPILOGUE

While the thrusting image of the Southern between the wars is recalled only by some senior citizens and old photographs, here and there a shabby relic survives in some forgotten corner. This concrete post and cast sign threatening trespassers with the majesty of the law – fine 40 shillings (£2) – lingered into the 1980s at Marchwood on the Totton to Fawley branch.

century or so of railway history, and also forward into the future. While my son and I continued our journey behind an Inter-City workhorse, first to Basingstoke, then later by a circuitous route that included the Eastleigh–Romsey section (not normally frequented by passenger trains) on board a WR diesel unit, the day was brought to a close with the 10.50 Penzance to Brighton service hauled by a brace of faithful 'Crompton' locomotives (33.022 and 33.046) that deposited us at Fareham at 17.09. The marathon begun at midnight had allowed us to sample a section of railway opened in 1840, be part of a centenary at Bournemouth and have unrestricted travel within the Runabout area on a peak day in every kind of train operated there. Contrasts, both with the past that I remember with so much affection, and between different parts of the same area in the eighties, stimulated the interest. Some places have changed almost out of recognition, while others have been touched more sympathetically by the passage of time. However much one might wish to restore the railway network to its former size and influence, the reality of life today cannot be ignored: at least there is a cohesive system, and it is still developing, as witness the Wessex electrics and the cross-country 'Sprinters'.

My advice to readers is to use, and enjoy, the railway as it is today in order that it can remain a valuable asset for tomorrow's generation. If, thereby, an interest is kindled in outworn technology and a respect for the achievements of yesteryear, then perhaps this book can serve a useful purpose with a nostalgic reminder for those halcyon days when the Southern stretched from Kent to Cornwall.

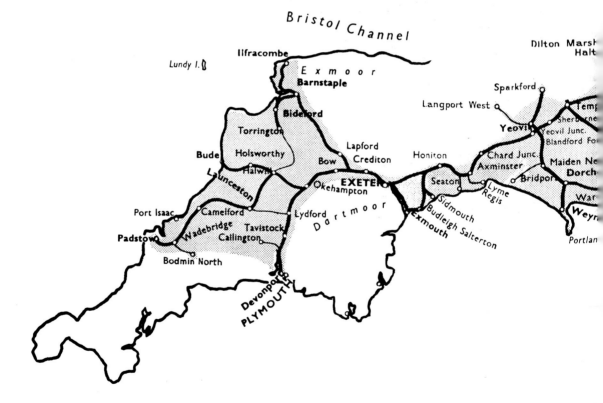